EP Sport Series

* All about Judo
  Backpacking
* Badminton
* Basketball
  Competitive Swimming
* Conditioning for Sport
  Cricket
  Field Athletics
* Football
* Golf
  Hockey for Men and Women
  Improve your Riding
  Learning to Swim
  Men's Gymnastics
  Modern Riding
* Netball
* Orienteering
  Rock Climbing
  Sailing
* Snooker
* Squash Rackets
  Start Motor Cruising
* Table Tennis
* Tennis up to Tournament
    Standard
* Track Athletics
  Trials Bike Riding
  Underwater Swimming
  Volleyball
  Water Polo
  Wildwater Canoeing
  Windsurfing
  Women's Gymnastics

At the time of publication of this edition the asterisked titles are available in paperback as well as hardback.

 EP PUBLISHING LIMITED

Present British Olympic team, 1980

ep sport

Weight Lifting

John Lear

Acknowledgements

ISBN 0 7158 0686 6 (cased)

Published by EP Publishing Ltd, East Ardsley, Wakefield, West Yorkshire, 1980

Text set in 11/12 Linotron Univers, printed by photolithography and bound in Great Britain by Redwood Burn Limited, Trowbridge and Esher.

The author and publishers would like to acknowledge with thanks the help of the following photographers in the preparation of this book: Leo Mason Sports Photography, for the cover picture; Oscar State, for the photographs specially taken at the European Championships in 1980 and appearing on pages 11, 17, 18, 27, 28, 85, 86; and George Kirkley, for all the other plates.

Contents

Introduction

Since the beginning of the evolution of man, his progress can be marked by testing his ability both physically and intellectually against others. Sport has developed as a result of these endeavours and tests of strength have always been an important way of displaying a man's superiority over his fellow beings. Throughout all history each civilisation has its stories and legends concerned with the great feats of strength and endurance of its heroes. Indeed, today those men who achieve the highest standards in sport prowess can be regarded as contemporary heroes demonstrating the power of youth and indeed may often be credited with demonstrating one nation's superiority over another. Weight lifting has developed from those days when men tested their strength by lifting and throwing stones and rocks, and the earliest sporting contests were very concerned with these types of activities and wrestling and running. Modern weight lifting, however, is very considerably changed since these early efforts and is now an activity which involves the athlete in most careful preparation if he is to achieve the best results. Modern weight lifting was held in the first Olympic Games of the modern era in 1896 and it was at this competition in Athens that Britain won its first, and only, Gold Medal when Launceston Elliot lifted 71 kg in the One Handed Lift. Weight lifting has changed a great deal since those days and I hope through this book to introduce you to a modern sport which will prove to be a fascinating challenge.

The sport today is controlled by the International Weight Lifting Federation and is truly international, and two lifts are selected for competition. These are the Two Hands Snatch and the Two Hands Clean and Jerk. Competitions are held at 10 body weight classes and range from club championships to World and Olympic Games. In competition the athlete is permitted three attempts at each lift and the best results on each lift are then added together to give a total. The lifter with the greatest total is the winner. This may sound simple enough but to reach the highest standards will demand that the athlete follows programmes that will develop great strength and speed, mastery of technique, great physical fitness, courage and above all a dedication and will to win.

The two lifts have been designed specifically to test special qualities within the athlete, but require considerable gymnastic skill coupled with power. In the first lift, the Two Hands Snatch, the weight is pulled from the floor directly to arms locked above the head. This requires the ability to develop great power. The lifter in moving under the bar can either sit down in the lowest position or split his feet fore and aft. These techniques are discussed later in the book. Weights well in excess of double body weight are handled in most classes.

The second of the lifts, the Two Hands Clean and Jerk, involves the lifting of the very heaviest weights. These are taken from the floor on to the lifter's chest in one continuous movement. Again the lifting action is combined with the lowering of the body so that the weight is caught on the chest. In order to do this, the lifter sits under the bar or again splits fore and aft to secure the weight on the chest. He must then recover from this low position to stand up. This in itself requires great determination and strength. The weight must now be driven above the head and held in a position under control until the referees of the competition give the signal to return the bar to the platform. As the lifter is only permitted three attempts at each of these lifts, a great deal of tension builds up with the competitions and the attention of the audience is always on the big scoreboards adding up the successful attempts of the snatch and clean and jerk, and working out what each lifter needs to take for his next attempt in order to try to improve his position within the competition.

As the competition develops, certain lifters are seen to be moving into positions of advantage. However, it is often the case that those who have produced a good result on the snatch may not be so good when they come to the clean and jerk and so their original leading position is under attack. On the other hand, a lifter who may have produced a poor result in the snatch is able, by determination and concentration, to lift very heavy weights in the clean and jerk, thereby re-establishing himself as a contender for the title of champion.

So the art of selecting the correct weights and ensuring that the lifter is correctly warmed up and ready to produce his maximum effort when called, is one of the main arts of coaching in the competition situation. The atmosphere in the warming-up room can be as electric as that on the actual competition platform.

Over the years the equipment used in the competition has improved considerably. Originally the old bar bells were of a solid construction and some of the sphere-type bar bells could only be adjusted in weight by adding lead-shot to the spheres. One can imagine, therefore, that many of the claims made for records were regarded with great suspicion. Some of the old bar bells used by the circus and music hall strong men were partially loaded with liquid mercury which would 'slop' about inside the sphere making it almost impossible to control them above the head.

With the advent of disc weight, however, bar bells could be made to weigh very accurately

Andy Drzewiecki

and this weight could be seen by the referees to be correct. Later a bar bell was developed that would revolve within its outside sleeves, thereby making the lifting of the weight on to the chest or above the head very much easier. The present international bar bell is a splendid piece of engineering. It is also very expensive and is not generally the sort of equipment that an individual would own but is, of course, to be found in all weight lifting clubs and many sports centres.

Lifting is now performed upon a platform which measures 4 × 4 metres. A good deal of stage setting is involved in modern competition with the platform, scoreboard and national flags at one end of the hall on a raised area and all brightly lit. Into this atmosphere steps the lifter, all his concentration focused upon overcoming the bar bell that lies before him. Now he must combine his strength and speed with the techniques and skills and great courage for which he will have prepared by many years of hard and dedicated training.

This book will introduce you to the techniques and training methods involved in the sport.

Accept the challenge of competition and as you win so you will improve. There is no limit in our sport, but weights which were considered impossible some years ago are now easily overcome by many lifters. You will, however, need help in reaching the highest levels. Join a club that has good training facilities and a coach.

Equipment

Apparatus

Weight lifting is performed on a bar bell which uses disc weights which range from 50 kg down to 1½ kg. In this way a comprehensive range of weights can be made up at 2½ kg intervals. Smaller weights down to ½ kg are also available for use at record attempts.

The bar bell itself, without any weights or collars, weighs 20 kg. This bar bell is constructed so that the bar revolves from inside the end sleeves. This makes for easier lifting and the bar is precision built to ensure accuracy and exact weight. Knurling provides a good gripping surface. These bar bells and weights are very expensive and few individuals will own such apparatus, but the majority of

clubs will have a fully comprehensive range of weight lifting apparatus. Lifts themselves must be performed in competition on a platform measuring 4 square metres. These are generally

made of wood, and rubber insets are included in the construction where the weight rests on the platform. These platforms, because of their heavy construction, are not generally movable and

Equipment: bar, discs, stands

therefore the club will provide a room specially for weight lifting.

In addition to this international bar bell, other pieces of apparatus will be used especially for assistance exercises. These will include dumb-bells, which are weights that can be used in each hand. Squat stands and racks which are height-adjustable will also be provided. These are used when it is necessary to support heavy weights as in the performance of many leg and overhead exercises. Adjustable benches, inclined abdominal boards and leg pressing machines will also prove to be of value.

Personal Equipment

My advice to any young weight lifter starting out on the sport is that the first item of personal equipment he should buy is a satisfactory pair of weight lifting boots. These will provide a flat, stable contact with the floor. As you will see from reading this book, balance is of the utmost importance and the boots must provide a non-slip surface. Secondly, the lifter should purchase a training suit that is warm. This will be worn during training and in warm-ups prior to competition and must be of such quality as to ensure that the lifter does not chill between his sets and warm-up exercises.

Certain rules are laid down as regards to the clothing worn in

Equipment: boots

competition. Generally this is a leotard or special costume which must be of one plain colour. A T-shirt with short sleeves may be worn underneath it and club or national insignia may be worn on this costume. Many lifters wear a belt. This piece of equipment is not so important nowadays as it was when the press was one of the competition lifts but many lifters feel the need to have this tight form of strapping about

Equipment: bar and discs

the waist. However, it must not exceed the width of 10 cms. All other personal equipment that the lifter wears on the platform is subject to the regulations of the International Weight Lifting Federation and will be checked by the referee at the weigh-in prior to the competition.

As fitness training is now an important part of the preparation, track shoes and extra track suits and T-shirts will be valuable. Remember that at all times it is essential to keep warm whilst training, for whether you are lifting heavy weight or performing power or endurance fitness training, the musculature of the body will be under considerable stress. All equipment must be kept thoroughly clean and in good repair.

Redzeb Redzhebov (Bulgaria) World Junior Featherweight Champion

Weight Lifting Terminology

In the weight lifting literature throughout the world, certain terminology is accepted. These terms are understood at all levels and will be used in this book under the two main headings of *technical training* and *training methods*.

Technical Training

Classical Lifts
The classical lifts are the Snatch and the Clean and Jerk and are those used in competition at all levels.

Snatch
This is the first of the two classical lifts, in which the bar bell is lifted over the head on two straight arms in one continuous dynamic movement. The body is lowered under the bar using either the split or squat technique.

Clean and Jerk
Second of the classical lifts in which the heaviest weights are lifted. This is a two stage lift in which the bar is first lifted on to the chest. The lifter may split or squat underneath the bar in this first part of the movement. Having then stood up, the lifter jerks or drives the weight to arms' length over the head and may split his feet in lowering his body under the bar.

Attempts and Total
The lifter is permitted 3 attempts at each lift. Between his first attempt and second attempt the minimum increase permitted is 5 kg, between his second and third attempt the minimum increase permitted is 2½ kg. The best result from the snatch and clean and jerk attempts are added together to give a total. The lifter with the best total is declared the winner of the competition.

Body Weight Classes
There are ten body weight categories. These are as follows:

Up to	52 kg
	56 kg
	60 kg
	67½ kg
	75 kg
	82½ kg
	90 kg
	100 kg
	110 kg
Over	110 kg

The lifter must weigh-in within the limits of his class.

Starting Position
Starting position is considered to be the position of the lifter at the moment the bar leaves the platform. This moment may commence from a static start where the lifter is motionless prior to lifting the weight or as a part of a dynamic start where the lifter has performed some preliminary movements to assist in overcoming the inertia of the bar bell. This is sometimes referred to as a rocket start and will be explained in greater detail later.

Pull
This refers to the lifting of the bar from the platform to a position of maximum extension prior to the drop. This word is unsatisfactory as the general understanding of pulling implies the bending of the arms.

Maximum Upward Extension
The lifter has made a maximum effort to lift the bar as high as possible with the full extension of the legs, body and shoulders at the top of the pull.

Lifting from the Hang
Here the bar is held in various positions such as knee height or mid thigh, and from a static start the lifter then completes the movement.

Lifting from Blocks
Similar to the hang but the lifter takes the weight from blocks of varying heights and completes the movement. Both lifting from the hang and lifting from blocks require very careful coaching as there is a tendency to try to overcome the inertia of the bar by throwing the shoulders backwards and 'leaning on it'.

Split-Drop
The lifter lowers or drops his body under the weight by splitting the legs fore and aft.

Squat-Drop
The lifter lowers or drops his body under the bar by sitting down in a squat position under it. The feet are jumped out to the side and the knees are turned out.

Snatch Grip
The width of grip suitable for snatching of weights.

Clean and Jerk Grip
Width of grip suitable for cleaning and jerking the weight. Means of deciding the width of grip for snatch and clean and jerk will be discussed later.

Normal Grip
Fingers wrapped round the bar with thumb outside fingers.

Hook Grip
Here the thumb is placed along the bar and the fingers are then wrapped round it squeezing it against the bar.

Knee Touch
Touching the knee on the platform during the execution of the split; this is cause for disqualification.

Elbow Touch
Touching the elbows on the knees in the squat clean; this is cause for disqualification.

Straps
Thongs of leather or webbing material coming from the lifter's wrists and wrapped around the bar thereby enabling the lifter to handle very heavy weights without fear of losing his grip.

Straps

Assistance Exercises

These fall into two categories: technical assistance exercises and power assistance exercises. Often parts of both are combined together and this will be illustrated and discussed under the chapter on assistance exercises.

Training Methods

Repetitions

The number of times an exercise or lift is performed without stopping.

Set

A group of a specified number of repetitions. Examples: 3 sets of 5 repetitions is written thus: 3×5.

Schedule

A plan of prescribed exercises showing sets, repetitions and weights to be handled.

Programmes

Composite plans directed towards a specific goal or competition. These may be of a long- or short-term nature.

Tonnage

Many schedules and training plans are based on tonnage principles. This is quite simple to follow and means the total amount of weight that is lifted in a training session. At different times of the year, depending on the distance from major competition, varying amounts of tonnage may be handled in each workout. The tonnage may also vary in certain plans from one workout to another within the week. In order to find out the tonnage for each workout you must add up everything that you lift in that workout: that will be all the weights multiplied by the repetitions for each set. At the conclusion you will have a figure of so many tons or metric tonnes.

Volume

The quantity of work done in a workout, which may be expressed in terms of number of lifts. This is very closely related to tonnage.

Intensity

To find the average intensity at which you have been working you divide the workout tonnage by the total number of repetitions for the workout. The same method can be employed to find out the intensity for each individual lift or exercise.

Tonnage stands for quantity – intensity stands for quality.

Mechanical Principles of Technique

Basic Principles

The objective of weight lifting is to exert maximum force against maximum resistance thereby overcoming it in certain prescribed technical movements. These technical movements refer to the two lifts used in international competition, the snatch and the clean and jerk. In order that these lifts may be performed successfully, the weight lifter and his coach will be concerned with the development of physical, technical and psychological preparation which involves a thorough understanding of the technical and tactical implications of the sport.

In this book we shall be concerned mainly with the technical development of the lifter from those learning stages as applied to the beginner and in the development of training methods, hopefully to achieve satisfactory results. The basic principles of technique are standard to all weight lifters irrespective of their size. These techniques relate to mechanical principles and unless there is some basic alteration of the rules to the sport they are unlikely to change in any marked degree. Basically, we are concerned to lift the greatest weights above the head either in a single stage movement, as in the snatch, or in a two stage movement, as in the clean and jerk. This means, as previously stated, the ability to exert maximum force to overcome the resistance or inertia of the weight. This will require great mechanical efficiency especially in the following three important areas:

1. Maximum power development.
2. Balance.
3. The ability to follow the line of least resistance.

The latter two are of special importance in the development of technique and it is necessary to develop a correct understanding of the basics of this technique from the very earliest days of a lifter's training. Before looking at the technique of each lift in detail, it is important to study the problems of balance and mechanics in a little more detail. Often the positions that the lifter must pass through during a lift are not those which would seem to be natural in endeavouring to exert maximum force. The difficulty, however, is that often those

Garry Langford, British Champion, snatches 150kg at the European Championships 1980

Minelio Pashov (Bulgaria)
World Junior Lightweight Champion
1980, with a world record jerk
of 183kg

movements that seem to be natural, such as endeavouring to lean one's body weight against the resistance as in the tug-of-war, are wrong and lead to serious errors in technique that once initiated can not be corrected. As already stated it is essential that correct technique should be understood and taught from the beginning of a lifter's career. This is the duty of both the coach and the lifter to adopt a disciplined approach to all training regimes. Remember that an experienced lifter may also become victim to the errors that the handling of very heavy weights may present. Bad habits, once formed, cannot be easily broken and it is frustrating that even after much correct coaching, when faults may appear to have been eliminated, there is always the danger that a lifter would, under stress and pressure, revert to the first thing learned. If his early training has been poorly constructed, this will possibly be a mistake.

Olympic lifting is unlike many other power activities in that due to the increase in weight between attempts, the circumstances change dramatically: e.g. it may be necessary, in order to win a competition, to attempt weights which the lifter has not approached before, e.g. in a World Championships, in order to secure first place, the competitor may be compelled to take world record attempts. Under such circumstances the techniques of the lifter must not fail him. It is an unfortunate fact that many lifters do not achieve the full potential that their strength levels would indicate due to a poor or undeveloped technical ability. Some lifters, on the other hand, because of their great fighting spirit and determination, become champions despite their poor technique. It should be the objective of the coach to produce the complete weight lifter by marrying together high standards of technical ability with a progressively developing programme of power training.

As mentioned earlier, we are concerned with the mechanical principles of balance and least line of resistance. Balance is the most important aspect of any skilled activity and unless we understand the principles of this and the least line of resistance we may not be able to employ our strength in the most effective manner. We should now look at these aspects in a little more detail.

Balance

Every object has a centre of gravity and as long as this centre of gravity falls within the base of the object, it will be said to be in balance. With regular objects it is easy to determine where the centre of gravity may be but when, as with the human body, the shape may be changed, then determining the point of the centre of gravity will be more difficult. When the human body is at the position of attention the centre of gravity will be within the body at approximately navel height and this will fall vertically over the feet. In this example, the feet, from toe to heel, are the base and as long as the centre of gravity is within that base, the individual will remain in balance.

If the lifter leans forward from the ankles, the centre of gravity will shift towards the toes and as long as this remains over the base the lifter is still in balance, but once he leans too far forward and the centre of gravity falls outside the base then he will fall over. Clowns in the circus will lean forward at very acute angles. This is permitted because they wear extremely large shoes and, of course, with this increase in base their forward angle can be very much greater.

It is important to remember that once a lifter is out of balance, his chances of effectively utilising his strength diminish very rapidly. In the sport of judo, the objective is to get one's opponent out of balance for then he becomes ineffective. Similarly, a boxer cannot throw an effective punch if he himself is out of balance. Similar problems exist when the base is seriously diminished in size. Consider the ballet dancer on her 'points' and many of the movements that the gymnast has to go through: in women's gymnastics, one of the pieces of apparatus – the beam – is designed purely to test the control of the gymnast under difficult balance conditions. The lifter, similarly, changes the position of his centre of gravity in relation to his base

and indeed at the top of the pull, when he is up on his toes, his base has diminished considerably. His problem is further complicated by the fact that he is endeavouring to deal also with an object other than his own body. This is, of course, the bar bell. Whenever there are two objects connected together, we are then concerned with the combined centre of gravity.

Combined Centre of Gravity

Assume that the weight lifter has stepped up to the bar bell, has grasped it in his hands and is in the starting position, preparing himself to make the lift. At this stage, we can talk about the centre of gravity of the lifter and centre of gravity of the bar bell as separate entities, but the moment that the lifter begins to exert force and lift the bar from the floor, we are then concerned with the combined centre of gravity of the bar bell and the lifter.

In the diagram which follows, the centre of gravity is always shown towards the heavier part of the object. In this case, with

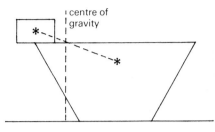

Once the combined centre of gravity falls outside the base, balance is lost

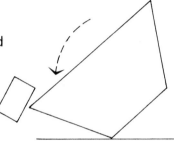

the up-turned 56 lbs, the centre of gravity is closer to the top than to the bottom, but falls over the centre of the base. When we add a small metal container to the one corner of the 56 lbs weight, the centre of gravity of this cup and the weight are now combined and this combined centre of gravity will move towards the cup, this now being the heavier corner of the weight. As material is added to the cup, thereby increasing the weight at that end, so the combined centre of gravity will move further up and towards the cup until eventually it will fall outside the base of the 56 lbs and the whole will topple over. Now, this simple diagram illustrates a similar condition of the lifter and the bar bell. When the lifter places his feet under the bar and bends down to grasp it, the forward angle of the shins from the ankle joint and the height of the bar bell from the floor force the bar bell to lie over the foot at a point where the toes and the body of the foot are joined. This, in fact, is towards the front of the base (toe to heel). Assuming that the lifter is reasonably proficient then the bar bell will be likely to be greater than his own body weight, and in some cases very much greater.

As explained before, the moment the lifter takes the bar from the floor we are concerned with combined centre of gravity and now the combined centre of gravity will be towards the heavier part of the object, i.e. the bar bell, and there will be a strong tendency for the lifter to be pulled off balance towards his toes. This will prevent him from exerting maximum force at the crucial point when he is endeavouring to overcome the inertia of the bar bell.

It becomes obvious, therefore, that the bar cannot be lifted in a vertical line from the floor but must be brought back towards the lifter at this stage, in order to bring the combined centre of gravity of bar and lifter over the centre of his base. This being achieved the lifter maintains his balance and, therefore, his ability to use effectively his power. The lifter is, therefore, taught to ease the bar back in towards the shins as it is lifted

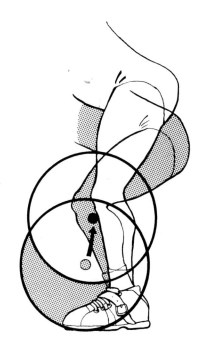

from the floor, so that by the time it is at knee height it is over the centre of his base. This is a deliberate technical instruction to the lifter and one can see that this technique is based upon sound mechanical principles. This is but one example of the understanding that makes up the total technical development in our sport.

Least Line of Resistance

In endeavouring to overcome the inertia of any heavy object, one of the simplest forms of machine that can be used is the lever. In the next illustration, the weight that has to be moved is greater than the strength potential of the lifter. By placing a long rod under one corner of the weight and another object in the centre of this rod, called the fulcrum, the lifter, by exerting force at the opposite end of the lever, will expect to be able to move the weight.

The distance between the weight and the fulcrum is called the weight-arm and the distance between the fulcrum

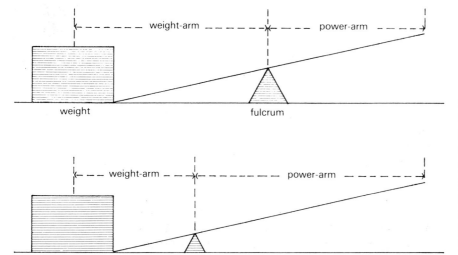

Greater mechanical efficiency is obtained by moving the fulcrum to the weight, thereby reducing the weight-arm

and the point where the force or power is exerted is called the power-arm. If in our example the weight weighs 100 units and the force exerted at the power of point is also 100 units, then the lifter will be unable to move the object for it will be necessary to exert a greater force at the point of power. This can be achieved by following progressive training programmes, thereby increasing the power potential of the athlete: for example, with the technically limited movement of the dead-lift, the lifter may be able to lift, as an absolute maximum, 500 lbs. In order to do more than this he must follow a sound training programme and hopefully be able to lift 520 lbs. In this way, by training, his success in this lift will be increased.

If we can go back to our first example, it may not be possible for an increase at the power point. However, by moving the fulcrum closer to the weight, the critical weight-arm is reduced and so much greater mechanical efficiency can be developed.

In human body/weight lifting terms, the weight is the bar bell. The levers are represented by the long bones of the body and the spine. Whilst the spine is made up of a number of bones, we shall consider it as a solidly constructed area, as a flat strong back is coached in all weight lifting movements. The joints are the fulcrums and the points of power are the areas where the muscles are attached to the bones. In all weight lifting movements where the objective is to develop as much mechanical efficiency as possible, the fulcrums or joints are always moved towards the weight. Any attempt to move the weight towards the fulcrums sets up paths of directions both for bar and body which make correct technical lifting extremely difficult to achieve. Remember the weight is heavier than you and it can very easily take control.

In the drawing on the facing page, the bar bell has been lifted to knee height and at this point of the lift it is moving through an area of mechanical and anatomical disadvantage. This area is called the Middle Range and in all weight lifting and weight training movements, one always encounters greatest difficulty in this area. At this particular point, since there are several fulcrums in operation, i.e. ankle, knee, hip and shoulder joints, we must decide which, in fact, is the *active fulcrum* which must be moved towards the weight. Since the legs are virtually straight, the choice lies

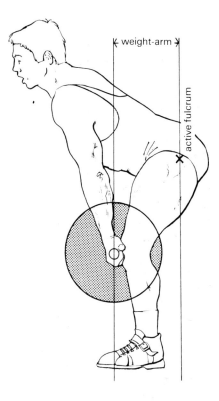

weight-arm

active fulcrum

×

consequence to pull the bar backwards thereby making control very difficult. It also limits the upward lifting potential. Here is an example where the natural movement that the lifter wishes to perform is, in fact, a serious mistake. The active fulcrum is, therefore, the hip joint. This joint must be forced in and upwards towards the weight thereby reducing the weight-arm between the joint and the vertical line of resistance. This allows the lifter to achieve a position of maximum upward extension thereby permitting him to exert maximum lifting force for the longest effective time. The shoulders will be seen to move from their forward position when the bar was at knee height to a position over the bar at the top of the pull. This backward movement is a reaction to the action of the forward hip drive. Lifters are given the coaching advice 'get your hips in' or 'force your hips in and up to the bar'. In fact, what the coach is telling the lifter to do is 'reduce the weight-arm that exists between the fulcrum and a vertical line through the weight by forcing the fulcrum in and upwards

towards the weight, thereby reducing the weight-arm and therefore obtaining the greatest mechanical efficiency'. I have here dealt with two principle technical considerations of balance and mechanical efficiency and it is upon these and other examples of simple mechanics that the technique of the two lifts is built.

between moving the shoulders back, or hips in and up, towards the vertical line through the weight.
Let us take the first choice of the shoulder joint. In endeavouring to straighten out the body against the resistance, it would seem natural to pull the shoulders back strongly. Unfortunately, this action causes the lifter to lean away from the bar and in

Technique of Classical Lifts

General Principles

The technique of the snatch and the clean and jerk is based upon the mechanical principles that we have discussed previously in combination with the physical qualities of agility, high degree of flexibility and the ability to express very high degrees of power. It must also be remembered that technique should not be considered in isolation as a mechanical phenomenon only but that these other physical elements are essential in its mastery. Whilst some lifters may be technically very efficient but comparatively weak and others very strong but technically inefficient, neither will achieve the highest possible results. So it is important to realise that technical development is an on-going process and that whilst there are certain basic standard technical essentials, as one develops and is able to lift greater and greater weights the implications change. In putting the shot, for example, the athlete – though he may encounter variations in throwing surface, weather conditions and so on – is still only concerned with the 16 lb weight for all his attempts. The weight lifter, however, although he too may encounter various qualities of platform, different makes of bar bell and changing environment between one weight-lifting hall and another, has in addition to overcome the very considerable problems of changing resistance between all his attempts. Now it may be necessary for him to enter into entirely unknown areas where he may be expected to establish new records in order to win the competition. It is at such times that the lifter's technique must not break down and that his previous training must ensure that he is able to exert maximum force on a background of sound and unchanging technique.

In many other aspects the weight lifter and shot putter require very similar physical attributes but in this one area of 'changing circumstance' the lifter has greater problems. As with other highly technical athletic activities it is the duty of the coach in dealing with beginners especially to insist that a correct technique is learnt from the very earliest stages and is then maintained and developed throughout the weight lifter's career.

Many lifters are far stronger than their technical abilities will permit them to demonstrate. In weight lifting terms, the easy part lies in 'getting strong'. The difficult part is being able to relate that strength to the highly athletic activities that are demanded by the snatch and the clean and jerk.

There are certain basic similarities between the snatch and the clean and these can be broken down into three basic stages of the lift:

1. Starting position leading to full extension; this is referred to as the pull.
2. Transitional movement.
3. Receiving position.

Similarly, with the jerk where the bar is driven from the chest above the head, we will be concerned with four basic stages:

1. Starting position.
2. The dip.
3. The drive.
4. The transitional drop to the receiving position.

Firstly, we will look at the snatch and clean in general terms.

The pulling movement and the receiving position are dynamic. To get from the starting position to that of maximum extension of the pull requires great power in overcoming the inertia of the bar bell. Here, we must develop acceleration on the bar: this means a steady and continuous build-up whereby muscle groups are used in sequence, the one building up on the other; this is called 'summation of force'. Here the object is to obtain maximum upward extension of the body so that the bar bell may be lifted as high as possible and that once the lifter begins to move to the receiving position, the momentum developed by a correctly executed pull will continue to cause the bar to accelerate upwards. Often this pulling movement is broken down into sections. These are referred to as first, second and even third pulls. To do this is incorrect for it gives the impression that the lifting of the bar is done in quite distinct sections whereas it must be a smooth and continually accelerating movement. For the purpose of theoretical analysis, we can sectionalise the movement. I shall refer to the pull by breaking it down into certain key positions but the coach should not convey this impression to the lifter. For instance, lifters have sometimes been told to lift the bar to the knee very slowly and then accelerate from that position. This acceleration is called the second pull but it has created great problems. If the bar bell is moving very slowly throughout the difficult position at knee height the only really effective means of then developing considerable speed is to throw the shoulders back and lean on the bar. The consequent technical errors can be disastrous. In coaching the lifter it is vital to convey to him that the pull is a smooth build-up of maximum force/efficiency.

The receiving position is one of great control and in order to ensure this, the lifter requires the mastery of those elements that make up great skill. Firstly, he must be very flexible in all the major joint complexes, in order that he may achieve the lowest possible positions as are demanded in the handling of maximum weights. Secondly, he must be very strong in this receiving position both to hold the weight and in the recovery. Thirdly, he must master the qualities of balance and bodily awareness. These are gymnastic qualities.

In many instances with the beginner, these receiving positions are difficult to achieve, and there are special technical assistance exercises to help overcome these difficulties and these are discussed and illustrated in the chapter on assistance exercises.

The transitional part of the lift refers to the change that takes place from the force-exerting position of the body in the pull to the force-controlling receiving position. This is also referred to as the drop. The body is weightless as the feet leave the ground and at this time can, therefore, have little or no control over the direction of the bar nor can it participate in the lifting of the bar to any greater height. Remember that the bar can only be lifted whilst the feet are in contact with the platform. The position that the lifter goes through during the drop will be very much controlled by the technique, satisfactory or otherwise, that has been adopted in the pull. It is obvious, therefore, that the pull will consequently effect the final receiving position and whilst mistakes may manifest themselves in the final

receiving position their origin will probably be in an error that has been made at some stage of the pull. For instance, it is easy to see that a lifter has dropped the bar behind his head in the squat snatch or that the split lifter has fallen to one side or other. All the audience will see these errors but the coach must be looking to see where they originated so as to be able to give *positive coaching advice* to eliminate the mistake at source. In order to do this effectively, two things must occur:

1. The coach must be able to give clear and simple advice.
2. The lifter must understand him.

All lifters must have basic theoretical knowledge of their sport in order for this to take place. This is an essential basic in the philosophy of coaching. Too often coaches give advice which is not easily understood and consequently not put into practice. The coach must try to impart understanding and not impress himself with his own rhetoric.

To this end it is important that the coach has a series of blueprints of correct technique in the back of his mind's eye

against which he will see and measure every lift. These blueprints refer to key positions. When you are coaching, try to make sure that the lifter is passing through these positions at all stages of the lift. Study them very carefully. As a lifter, you should try to develop a sense of how it feels to be in these positions at the various stages of the lift. Many of the assistance exercises will help with this development. These key positions are as follows:

For the Pull

1. Starting position. This refers to the exact moment when the bar leaves the platform. In watching lifters, you will see many different movements of the body take place prior to the lifting of the bar. With the exception of a few very advanced lifters these movements are generally only effective as a form of psychological winding up prior to exerting maximum effort.

2. The bar at knee height. It is essential that the lifter and bar move through the correct path

David Rigert (USSR) in the process of jerking
227.5kg

Pavel Pavlov (Bulgaria), World Junior Light Heavyweight Champion, snatching 160kg

at this very difficult position. It is a difficult area because it is the Middle Range where the lifter is suffering from both mechanical and anatomical disadvantage. Mechanically the weight-arm between the active fulcrum of the hips and the vertical line through the bar is most difficult to overcome at this stage. Anatomically there is a change-over from those muscles which straighten the leg to those which extend the body at the hip. Wherever there is such an anatomical change-over there is a weak link.

3. Full extension at the top of the pull. In order that momentum is developed the lifter must aim for this full extension. However, this does not mean that the pull is continued indefinitely for there is a critical point where the lifter must change to the drop for the receiving position.

4. Transitional period or drop. As we have seen the position of the body in this area will be dependent to a great degree upon the pull and will consequently affect the receiving position.

For the Jerk

1. Starting position. Here the lifter has recovered from the clean and is standing in a positive and dynamic position.
2. The dip. The position achieved during this movement will determine the success, or otherwise, of the jerk to a very great degree.
3. The drive. This is a dynamic upward thrust against the bar which gives a limited upward impulse with maximum weights.
4. The receiving position. Here the lifter has dropped under the bar using a high split and should be seen in a position of strong support under the bar. All these key positions for pulls, receiving positions and for the jerk will be discussed in greater detail but it is important to remember at this stage that a lifter may not pass through or achieve these positions properly due to any or all of the following:
1. Lack of strength in any of the essential muscle groups working at any stage of the lift. Wherever such muscular weakness exists there will be a fall-off in the total efficiency of the movement.

2. Loss of balance. We have discussed this earlier in some detail but remember that if the lifter is out of balance he will not be able to utilise effectively the power that is at his disposal.
3. Use of the wrong muscle groups at the wrong time, i.e. lack of co-ordinated muscular effort. This often results from bad coaching at the earliest stages: e.g., the lifter may be allowed to bend his arms far too early in the lift. This attempt at 'snapping' at the bar will lead to out-of-sequence muscle group effort and a considerable diminishing of efficiency.
4. Lack of full joint mobility. Essential positions cannot be achieved unless the lifter is fully flexible. Muscular injury is also limited when a condition of full flexibility is achieved. Remember the condition of being 'muscle bound' does not exist for the Olympic weight lifter.
5. Especially as a result of No. 1, but also for all the reasons outlined above, the lifter may find great difficulty in development of speed. Remember that whilst we agree that there may be some slow-moving strong men there have certainly never been any fast-moving weak men.

Double Knee Bend Phenomenon

The action of leaning against the weight causes the lifter to jump away from the bar and in addition transfers the effort on to directing the bar bell backwards. It becomes impossible to control the path of a heavy bar bell under these circumstances. This is a cardinal mistake in weight lifting but is understandable in that the lifter, in endeavouring to overcome the resistance, uses his body weight in the same way as a participant in tug-of-war leans backwards against the rope. In addition full extension is prevented and the reaction is for the feet to jump forwards as the shoulders go backwards. Since these errors result from moving the fulcrum of the shoulders backwards to the vertical line through the weight, then it must be the hip joint which is to be moved. The hip joint, therefore, becomes the *active fulcrum* and must be driven in and upwards towards the weight. This action reduces the weight-arm, develops acceleration on the upward path of the bar bell, and allows those muscles which extend

the body into the upright pulling position to work at their maximum efficiency.

In watching the lifter whilst this movement is being performed, it will be observed that the shoulders do, in effect, move backwards. This movement, however, is a reaction to the forward action of the hip joint. Nevertheless, the lifter is still coached to try to keep his shoulders forwards as long as possible so that at the top of the pull he is in an upright lifting position over the bar. During these first two stages of the lift the knees will be seen almost to straighten and then to rebend as the hips are driven in. This is an *anatomical accident* and is not a coachable technique. However, confusion in analysing the mechanics and anatomy involved has led to serious coaching errors. This phenomenon, known as the Double Knee Bend, is seen to occur during a phase of the pull between key position Nos. 2 and 3. If the bar bell has been lifted from the floor correctly, utilising the major muscles of the legs, it will be seen that when it reaches key position No. 2 at knee height the legs at the knee joint are virtually

straight with the lifter flat on his feet having maintained the angle of the back.

From this position the lifter must endeavour to achieve a position of upward maximum extension. This requires that the active fulcrum of the hips be driven in and upwards towards the vertical line through the bar bell. At the same time as the lifter achieves this final position he will be rising up on his toes. It is during this phase of the movement that the knees bend and move forwards for a second time. Ultimately this second bending of the knees will be of advantage to the lifter as it gives him an extra 'kick' upwards thereby giving extra acceleration to the bar bell at the top of the pull. Since this is seen to be advantageous, a deliberate bending and pushing forwards of the knees has been coached. The real action, however, is as stated an anatomical accident.

Study of simple anatomy and kinetics of this stage of the movement will show that those muscles which extend the hip joint also flex the knee and the muscle which helps the lifter to rise up on his toes in a load-bearing position also flexes the knee. This strong action at the hip and ankle joint causes knee bending and whilst, as explained, it is advantageous to the lifter, it is accidental. Here is an anatomical analysis of this action.

Extension of the Hip and Flexion of the Knee

Muscles in action:
Biceps femoris, long head from tuberosity of Ischium (base of pelvis) to lateral head of tibia and fibula.
Semi tendinosus from tuberosity of Ischium to upper part of the inner surface of tibia.
Semi membranosus from tuberosity of Ischium to posterior surface of back of head of tibia.
This group of muscles is commonly referred to as the ham-string group and comes strongly into play in all lifting movement.

Extension of the Ankle Joint and Flexion of the Knee

Gastrocnemius from heel bone via the Achilles' tendon to posterior aspect of femur (back of knee joint).
This muscle is a prime mover for plantar flexion of the ankle joint when in a load-bearing position. It is a true flexor of the knee joint.
Mistaken coaching of a deliberate second knee bend will result in the following:
1. The lifter comes forwards on to his toes too soon.
2. The knees, being bent far too early, are pushed forwards. These two errors together result in loss of balance.
3. There is a lowering of the body with a consequent diminishing of upward lifting force on the bar bell and also an exaggerated forward displacement of the bar.

Two Hands Snatch

Grip

The first thing that we must consider is the difference between the width of grip employed in the two hands snatch and that used for the clean and jerk. In performing the two hands snatch the weight must be taken from the ground to above the head in one movement, whilst lowering the body under the bar, either by means of the squat technique or the split technique.

In the early days of modern weight lifting it was realised that the wider the grip on the bar bell the lower the height it had to be lifted, and so many lifters employed extremely wide grips with their hands touching the inside collars of the bar bell. Whilst an advantage in terms of lower height for the bar to be lifted

could be obtained, the great disadvantage was that the wider grip diminished the force potential of the pull, for it was well known that the most efficient pulling position was with the hands at shoulder width apart.

Considering the two requirements of lesser height and strongest possible pull,

basic principles of mechanics had to be employed to arrive at a satisfactory and effective position for the hands on the bar bell. This is achieved in the following way. The lifter, standing erect, holds the upper arms horizontal. The distance from elbow joint to elbow joint across the back is measured and is then marked on the bar

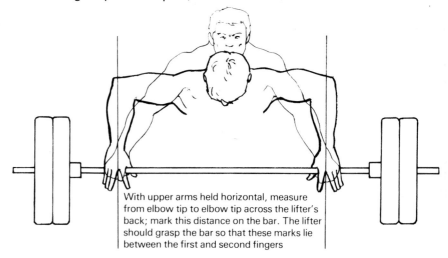

With upper arms held horizontal, measure from elbow tip to elbow tip across the lifter's back; mark this distance on the bar. The lifter should grasp the bar so that these marks lie between the first and second fingers

bell with chalk. The lifter then grips the bar so that these marks lie between the first and second fingers. The mechanical principles involved here are as follows.

Accepting that the wide grip means lesser height to pull the bar, we are confronted immediately by the problem of a weight-arm existing between a vertical line through the shoulder joint and a vertical line through the point where the hands grip the bar bell. The closer the grip the less will be this weight-arm. By holding the upper arm horizontal to the ground a weight-arm exists between the elbow joint and the shoulder joint with the forearms hanging vertically that will be the limit of this particular disadvantage. Should the hands be taken out wider than this, the weight-arm will increase and the ability to exert maximum force diminish. It is, however, possible to have a slightly narrower grip and obtain greater advantage, but the ability to use this will depend greatly upon the flexibility of the upper spine of the lifter.

Starting Position

The feet should be approximately hip width apart with the toes turned slightly outwards for comfort. As most people walk with their feet turned slightly outwards this is permitted but it should not be taken to the extreme. The nearer the feet can be positioned to pointing fore and aft, the better for the final drive at the position of maximum extension. In all driving and leaping movements final propulsion comes from the big toe and if the foot is turned outwards excessively, the effectiveness of this propulsive element is diminished. If the feet are too wide apart, then in the position of maximum extension high up on the toes, the direction of force will be crossing through the body and will consequently be less effective. A slightly wider than hip width for the feet is considered by some authorities to be more effective for the start of the lift when the bar is taken to knee height, but the complete pull must be taken into consideration and so the hip width stance is recommended.

In addition, the lifter must feel his body weight over all of his foot; he should not be either rocking back on his heels or feeling a forward pressure on to the front of his foot.

Bearing these points in mind, it is essential that a first-class pair of weight lifting boots are the priority purchase for a young lifter. Remember that as explained earlier we are very concerned with balance and a correctly designed boot, providing a strong firm base, is essential.

The feet are placed under the bar bell so that the bar lies approximately over the point of the foot where the toes and instep join. This means that when the lifter bends down, the shins will come forward to touch the bar in the starting position. If the feet are placed too far forward under the bar, the forward movement of the shins when the knees are bent will cause the bar bell to roll forward away from the lifter.

The grip is as described above and the lifter should employ the hook technique.

The back is flat and held in a strong position throughout the movement maintained by the muscles of the back and especially those which surround the vertebra. The knees are bent to an angle between 90° – 100°. Analysis of many lifters, over the years, has shown that despite varying body weight classes and sizes, the angle of the knees within these limits has been employed at the moment the bar bell leaves the ground. Often lifters perform other movements prior to lifting the bar. These are non-technical movements, generally performed in the psychological development of an energy build-up. This angle at the knee joint ensures that the hips are higher than the knees. This position combined with an attempt to keep the shoulders forward, as long as possible, throughout the lift helps to prevent the error of pulling back.

The elbows should be rotated outwards and the shoulders eased forward. This will prevent the arms from flexing too soon and ensure that when they do, as at the top of the pull, their line of direction will be vertical. The head should be set comfortably with the eyes looking down approximately 1½ metres in front of the lifter. Avoid the tendency to press the

Starting position (snatch): key position No. 1

head back and look up as this will cause the lifter to pull back. This then is the starting position or *key position No. 1*. Most beginners should be encouraged to see this as a 'get set' and to lift from this position without preliminary

movement. More advanced lifters able to exercise a little more control often go through preliminary movement, but at the very moment that the bar bell leaves the floor they too must be passing through the position as just described.

The Lift

In order to overcome the inertia of the bar bell the biggest and strongest muscles of the body must be used first. These are in the legs. This means that the back works statically to maintain the original starting position as the legs drive strongly against the resistance. The bar bell must be eased in and towards the shins. In the initial starting position when the bar was over the junction of the toes and the instep of the foot, it permitted the knees to bend so that the shins could come forward to touch the bar. This meant that the correct angle at the knee joint could be achieved so that the hips were not too low at the start of the movement. However, if the bar were lifted in a vertical line from this initial starting position, it would be too far forward towards the front edge of the base, i.e. the foot, and the tendency would be for the lifter to be pulled forwards and off balance.

Since maintaining balance will determine the effectiveness of the lifter's pulling power, the bar bell must be brought back to a position where the

Key position No. 2

combined centre of gravity of lifter and bar bell are over the centre of the base. The bar bell is then eased back in and towards the shins during this first stage of the lift to knee height. At the knee height position when the shins are

vertical the bar bell will be close to the knee and over the centre of the base. This easing in of the bar also causes the shoulders to come slightly forward. This in itself is of benefit as it helps to limit the desire to throw the shoulders back against the weight, especially in the middle position.

This first part of the lift is, therefore, a very vigorous drive of the legs and takes the lifter to *key position No. 2*, with the bar bell at knee height. As with all Middle Range movements, the lifter will encounter some of the greatest difficulties in the entire lift. This second key position finds the lifter struggling with the problems of mechanical and anatomical disadvantages. Mechanically, two major weight-arms affect this stage of the lift. These are:

1. The weight-arm between the fulcrum of the hip joint and a vertical line through the weight, and

2. Between the shoulder and the vertical line through the weight. As was seen earlier, to obtain maximum mechanical efficiency weight-arms must be reduced and this is done by moving the fulcrum towards the weight. Since we have two fulcrums, i.e. hip and shoulder, we must decide which is the *active fulcrum*.

Key position No. 3: we have seen that the *active fulcrum*, in achieving upward extension,

Key position No. 3

must be the hip joint. There is a subtle difference in the action of the hips between the two techniques of snatching. The emphasis changes slightly as follows.

For the squat style the hip action is *up* and in and for the split style the action is *in* and up. This means that the squat lifter emphasizes the upward component and the split lifter emphasizes a very strong inward component of the lift. As the hips are driven in and upwards towards the bar the lifter must endeavour to keep over as long as possible. This will ensure that the bar bell is lifted up.

In coaching it is often necessary to emphasise that the bar bell is lifted upwards and not backwards or forwards. This may sound rather obvious but unfortunately due to mechanical errors in technique the bar bell can be directed out of line with disastrous results. If the lifter has maintained the outward rotation of the elbows and the position of the shoulders described in the initial starting position, this upward action should be achieved.

The lifter will rise high on his toes with the hips in to the bar, the head driving upwards and the shoulders being lifted vigorously up towards the ears. The arms are allowed to bend slightly but it should be realised that vigorous attempts at lifting the bar by bending the arms prevent full extension and frequently result in the lifter folding up as he begins to move into the receiving position. From this position of maximum upward extension, the lifter moves through the transitional, or drop, part of the movement. This drop is slightly different between the squat technique and the split technique.

Squat Technique

Having reached the position of maximum upward extension the lifter jumps his feet outwards and to the side at the same time turning the knees outwards. It is important to maintain the position of the trunk upright. This means that the body position obtained in the final part of the extension must be maintained as the lifter drops underneath the bar. The action of turning the feet out and jumping them apart will allow the hips to come close between the heels and allow the upper two-thirds of the trunk to remain upright. The coach is often heard to instruct the lifter to 'sit in and sit up.' The upright position of the upper two-thirds of the trunk places the lifter in the strongest position to punch out against the resistance of the bar as he moves under it. This is the strongest receiving position. Lifters who have leant backwards on the bar will then have to counteract this error by

Squat technique: the drop

throwing the head and shoulders forwards and flicking the bar behind the head. This is a weaker position and, of course, often causes considerable problems in controlling the direction of the bar bell. The lifter must train to drop into the lowest possible receiving position and the bar bell at arm's length will be directly above the shoulders and placed over the effective centre of the base. This is the essential position of balance. Remember that with the bar bell held high above the head the centre of gravity will be higher, and so balance in a backward/forward plane will be critical.

When the lifter starts to move his feet from the ground to jump them into the final receiving position the bar bell should continue to rise on the momentum imparted to it by correct extension of the body during the pull. Any action of the arms pulling against the bar will in fact result at this stage of the movement in accelerating the lifter's descent under the bar. This is to the lifter's advantage.

As the lifter reaches the final receiving position underneath the bar bell the bar, which will be slightly in front of the lifter, must be eased backwards. This movement must be checked as the bar comes over the lifter by driving vigorously upwards with the heels of the hand. The final receiving position as shown on this page is a very strong position for supporting heavy weight, but remember that balance must be controlled to achieve this position.

In order to recover from the final low position of balance, the lifter should ease his head through the arms slightly, at the same time lifting the hips upwards. This action will help to relieve pressure on the tightly compressed knee joints, giving those muscles, which extend the knee, a more favourable angle of pull at the start of the movement. Arms, however, must remain vertical, pressing strongly against the resistance. Because of the action of lifting the hips, the trunk will be slightly inclined forwards but this position will be kept to a minimum by keeping the knees out and apart during the recovery.

When the lifter has stood erect he should step his feet back into line in the hip width position

Final receiving position

and there await the signal from the referee to return the bar bell to the platform.

Split Technique

During the final drive into extension at the top of the pull, the split lifter must pay particular attention to driving the hips *in* and up towards the bar. This action will take the lifter down and forwards once the feet leave the ground. From the position of maximum upward extension the lifter comes off both feet at exactly the same time to split them fore and aft. It is essential that all those who employ this technique are coached to come off both feet together. Having said this, it is only fair to point out that in detailed study of all the great split lifters, the rear foot has always moved fractionally before the front foot. This is due to the following facts:

1. There are only some 15° of extension at the hip joint backwards.

2. However hard we try for a direct upward extension there is inevitably some slight lean back with maximum weights which causes the lifter to move the rear foot in order to be in a position to re-establish his balance.

3. The rear leg travels further and consequently needs to move faster.

At the highest level of lifting these phenomena will be basically subconscious and, as already explained, a very definite attempt must be made to ensure that the rear foot leaves the ground at the same time as the front foot. Lifters of a more limited standard are often seen to move the rear foot well before the completion of extension. The results of this error are:

1. The lifter is left pulling on one leg only and is consequently badly out of balance.

2. He can only exert force through the one leg (front leg) as that is the only part of the body in contact with the ground.

3. Because of the limited extension (15°) at the hip joint the body can be tilted forwards by throwing a leg back vigorously.

4. Any attempt at a hip swing in and upwards towards the bar will be killed. In fact, the hips can only be pulled back and twisted away from the line of the bar bell.

All these things combine to diminish seriously the lifter's ability to use his full power potential. For these reasons the split technique is now rarely used. However, some people – especially if they come to weight lifting a little later in their lives – may find that problems of flexibility, especially in the upper spine, will make satisfactory performance of the squat technique difficult, but it will still be possible for them to achieve first-class results using split technique, providing they pay very careful attention to detail and receive first-class coaching.

Assuming that the lifter has chosen to perform the split technique, let us consider the further technical requirements. Having reached maximum upward extension, the lifter comes off both feet together. The *inward* and upward action of the hips will now take the lifter forwards as he drops down underneath the bar bell. It is essential that he maintains the upright position of the trunk allowing the hips to lead him under the bar. No attempt should be made to push the head and shoulders forward as such a movement is quite unnecessary. The feet will come to land at approximately the same time although the rear foot may touch down fractionally before the front. The forward action of the hips will allow them to travel down and towards the front heel and the knee will travel forwards in advance of the ankle. The receiving position is very low. One of the reasons for disqualification is when the knee of the rear leg touches the platform. If the hip drive forwards and upwards has been allowed to continue there should be no danger of this occurring because the direction of force will be out over the front ankle and the forward knee. The action of the arms in moving under the bar is slightly different from that employed by the squat technique lifter. As the lifter is moving forward he is rotating the bar within its own axis and as the body comes beneath it, he must punch out vigorously with the heels of the hands. The balance in this receiving position is critical from side to side and displacement of the lifter or the bar bell in this direction causes serious problems of control. Of the two techniques, this is probably the more gymnastic and gives great satisfaction in correct performance. To recover from this low position (see right), the lifter must carefully tilt the bar bell backwards. This action will relieve pressure on the tightly compressed front knee joint; at the same time, stiffening the rear leg, he should push strongly with the front and step it in a short pace. By tilting the bar very slightly forward, the rear leg can then be brought into line with the front foot. Recovery in this way is important. Should the rear foot be moved before the front one, there is a tendency for the body to incline forwards and for

Split snatch: low position; the photograph shows Vorobyev (USSR), former World Champion, a great exponent of the split style of snatching

the lifter to begin to run towards the front of the platform. Many an otherwise successful lift has been lost because of faulty recovery. The techniques of weight lifting are very difficult to master and the more often you are confronted with the essential basic elements the more likely you are to perform the movements correctly and

achieve satisfactory results. The weight lifter must be a thinking athlete concerned at all times with developing technique. For this reason I include here, and also at the end of the sections on the clean and the jerk, a summary of those points which you must keep in your mind at all times.

Summary of Two Hands Snatch

Key Position No. 1 (starting position)

Feet: hip width apart, flat on floor
Knees: 90–100%
Back: flat but not vertical
Shoulders: slightly in advance of the bar
Head: in comfortable position, eyes looking down about 1½ metres in front of the lifter
Hands and arms: hook grip, elbows rotated outwards, shoulders brought forward. This is a dynamic position which the lifter must be in at the moment the bar leaves the ground.

Key Position No. 2 (bar at knee height)

Feet: flat on floor
Shins: vertical
Knees: naturally straight with bar close to the knee cap
Back: flat and still at approximately the same angle as at starting position
Shoulders: in advance of the bar
Arms: straight with elbows rotated out
Head: position maintained

Key Position No. 3 (maximum upward extension)

Feet: high on toes
Knees: legs straight
Hips: in close to the line of the bar bell
Arms: beginning to bend with a very strong elevation of the shoulders upwards towards the ears
Head: driving up

Key Position No. 4 (receiving position)

1. SQUAT
Feet: jumped out and apart, flat on floor
Knees: turned out and pointing over and in the same direction of the feet
Hips: will be set back in sitting position but close between the heels
Back: natural curve in lumbar spine as in sitting position but upper two-thirds of the trunk vertical
Arms: straight above the head with a strong elbow lock supporting the bar

2. SPLIT
Feet: split fore and aft, front foot flat on the floor with toe turned slightly inwards, rear foot on the ball of the foot with heel straight so that whole foot is directed to front
Knees: the front knee is bent and pushed forward over the front foot, the rear leg has very slight flexion at the knee joint but is strongly supportive
Hips: square to the front and close towards the front heel
Trunk: is maintained upright and the arms are locked and pushing vigorously against the bar bell above the head

Direction of the Bar during the Pull

The reader should study the diagram on the next page carefully. This illustration shows the correct line of pull, or trajectory, of the bar bell during the pulling movements as compared with the line of pull illustrated in two basic technical mistakes. Mechanically, it would seem logical that the bar should be lifted in a straight vertical line as the shortest distance between two points is a straight line. In practice, however, due to realistic mechanical/anatomical parameters the bar bell is lifted in a shallow S-shaped curve.

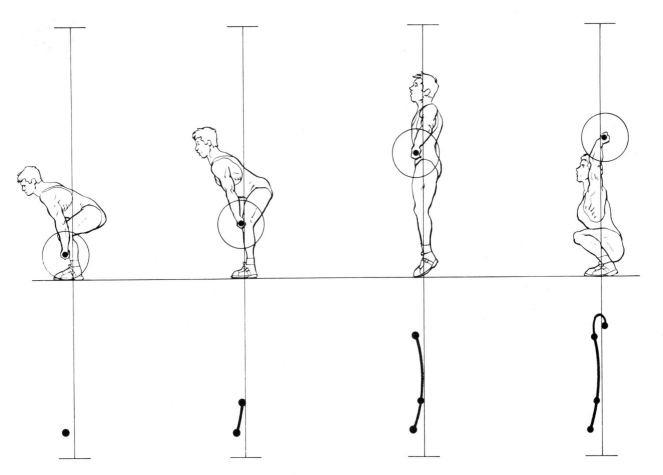

Starting position: bar towards front of base due to forward angle of shins

Bar at knee height: as legs straighten shins move back allowing bar to be eased in over centre of base

Full extension: bar carries slightly forward as hip fulcrum is driven in and up

Receiving position: bar is taken back slightly to bring it over the lifter

We have seen already that efficiency in overcoming the resistance relies upon using the most effective mechanical application and anatomical kinetic function.

The start of the movement requires that the bar bell is taken in towards the shins. This ensures that the combined centre of gravity of body and bar is over the centre of the base, ensuring balance and, therefore, placing the lifter in the most efficient position to bring anatomical and kinetic advantage into play. From the point where the bar is passing the knees, the lifter endeavours to lift the bar vertically. However, due to the inward and upward extension of the body, the bar carries forwards slightly. At the top of the movement there is a 'hook' on the bar to bring it above the head as in the snatch, or on to the chest as in the clean. Coaches should study this pathway carefully and see whether the lifter and bar are in correct relationship, especially at key position No. 2 when the bar is at knee height. Two basic errors are illustrated in the drawing on p. 44; the first shows the bar bell moving away from the lifter at the start of the movement. (Path D) This can be caused by:

1. The inexperienced lifter fearing that he will bang the bar against the knees which are set forward in the starting position and thereby subconsciously lifting the bar out and round the knees.

2. Assuming the position over the bar when the legs are straight with the bar bell pressed close to the shins; when the lifter then bends the legs in assuming the correct starting position, the bar bell is pushed forwards and rolls away from the lifter.

3. Starting the movement with the seat too low.

The action of the bar bell travelling forwards tends to pull the lifter off balance and on to his toes. The heavier the resistance the more likely this effect will be. When the lifter is off balance he can no longer exert maximum force. In addition there is an increased weight-arm when the bar travels forwards. The effect of this is for the lifter to pull the bar bell back vigorously and again this incorrect redirection of the bar becomes uncontrollable. The second technical mistake occurs when the backward movement of the bar bell is continued past the knees, pulling the bar bell in towards the hips. (Path C) This action results in either:

1. An exaggerated swing of the bar forwards in order to drive the hips in for a complete upward extension, *or*

2. A fixing of the hips with the shoulders being thrown back vigorously and the bar bell being pulled back.

Both these errors result in considerable mechanical and anatomical disadvantage for the lifter. He will be unable to utilise his power source to full advantage. When I am coaching, I try to stand at the side of the lifter so that I can observe the pathway of the bar bell in relationship to the positions that the lifter passes through. It is my experience that if the lifter and bar bell are in the correct relationship at key position No. 2 especially, then the chances of a successful lift are high. Coaches should make a careful study of the pathway of the bar as there are a number of variations on the rational shallow S-shaped curve which can affect, to a lesser or greater degree, the success, or otherwise, of the lifter.

The pathways, A, B and the solid line 1 marked in E, fulfil the basic criteria of line of direction for the pull. In figure E the dotted line 2 shows the bar to have been pulled forward usually due to an incomplete extension of the body, and in dotted line 3 the bar has been pulled back due to the lifter "leaning" backwards during the pull. The errors in direction of pull in C, D and E 2 and E 3 result in loss of momentum and less effective use of power sources.

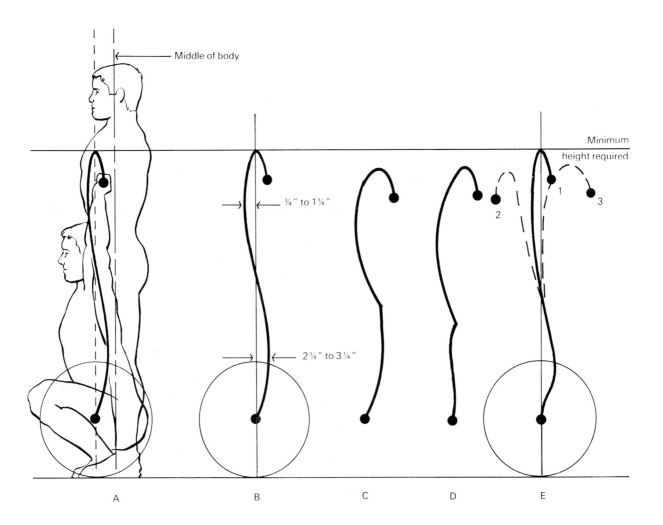

Middle of body

Minimum
height required

¾" to 1¼"

2¼" to 3¼"

1

2

3

A   B   C   D   E

Clean and Jerk

We shall now look at the second of the two classical lifts, the clean and jerk; but for the purpose of analysis we shall divide it into the two sections of (a) clean and (b) jerk. This is the second lift and for two reasons it is especially important in the competition.

1. The heaviest weights are handled and in consequence all the technical points that have been covered for the snatch must be emphasised, for remember that the increased resistance will be an extra problem that the lifter must deal with in maintaining his skill and technique.

2. As it is the final lift a good result is important. Often lifters have been required to break world records on the clean and jerk in order to take first place in the competition.

There are two techniques in the cleaning part of the lift when, similarly to the snatch, the lifter may employ the squat style or the split style; but in the jerk all lifters are taught to employ the shallow split. In modern training young lifters are taught the squat style clean.

The Clean

Squat Technique for Clean
Width of grip. The first major difference between the snatch and the clean will be observed in the selection of the width of grip. As was pointed out during the description of the snatch, the closer the width to shoulder width the stronger the pulling position. Lifters are, therefore, taught to grasp the bar with a shoulder width grip. This means that when the bar is lifted on to the shoulders the inside edge of the hand close to the thumb is level with the outside edge of the muscles of the shoulder.

In the receiving position, with the bar on the shoulders, the bar can rest across the top of the chest and the anterior portion of the shoulder joint. With the elbows held slightly upwards, this ensures that the bar is resting on a strong firm base from which it can be driven at the commencement of the jerk. The lifter must employ the hook grip technique.

Starting Position
The feet are placed hip width apart with toes turned slightly outwards and are positioned under the bar so that the vertical line through the bar cuts through the foot at the

Starting position (clean)

junction of the toes and the instep. The lifter must feel the weight of his body over all of his foot from toe to heel. This will ensure that he is in a balanced position when he starts to lift the bar from the ground. Assuming the shoulder width grip, as described above, the lifter, maintaining his back in a flat, strongly held position, flexes at the knees and hips thereby bending down so that he may grip the bar. The angle at the back of the knees is between 90–100°. This ensures that the hips are higher than the knees and due to the shoulder width grip, the angle between the chest and the front of the thigh will be more open than in the snatch. This is a more advantageous starting position.

The elbows are rotated outwards and the shoulders, which are slightly in front of the bar, are brought round and forwards. The arms are straight and the eyes look down and forwards about 1–1½ metres in front of the lifter. This is essentially a dynamic position in which the lifter gathers all his force potential which he must employ in overcoming the very heavy weight. Remember also that this is the position that the lifter must be in at the moment the bar leaves the floor. Whilst more advanced lifters may go through a series of preliminary movements, at the actual moment of lifting the bar they must achieve this position. We shall refer to this as *key position No. 1* and young lifters should be coached to start the lift from this position.

The Lift

In the starting position the lifter is coached to place his feet under the bar so that the bar is over the junction of the body of the foot and the toes. When he bends down to grasp the bar the shins will come forward to touch it. This starting position, however, means that the bar bell is forward to the front of the base. Should the bar be lifted in a vertical line the lifter, especially since the bar is now very heavy, would most certainly be pulled forwards off balance. In starting the weight from the floor two considerations, therefore, are of great importance:

1. That the bar and body are so positioned mechanically that greatest efficiency can be obtained.

2. As a result of this first consideration the largest and most powerful muscles of the body, i.e. in the legs and hips, may be brought into play to overcome the inertia of the bar bell.

It is essential, therefore, that as the bar bell is lifted from the floor and the shins move backwards as the legs are straightened, the bar must be eased in so that by the time it is at knee height it is over the centre of the foot. This will ensure that throughout the first stage of the lift, the lifter remains in balance.

Throughout this first stage of the lift, the back is maintained flat with the shoulders being held forwards.

The coaching of the first section of the clean is extremely important because it is at this stage, when the lifter endeavours to overcome the great resistance, that he may revert to manoeuvres which are contrary to the basic correct technique but which often seem and feel natural. One of the most serious mistakes is for the lifter to 'sit and lean' against the bar bell. Great discipline is required of the lifter to ensure that the shoulders are kept forwards over the bar bell throughout this early stage of the lift. This will be helped when the bar bell is eased back into the shins as the shoulders will come forward slightly as a reaction to this movement. When the bar is at knee height the lifter is said to be in *key position No. 2*. Coaches and lifters should have a very clear picture in their minds as to what this implies, as it is essential that the lifter and the bar bell are in correct relationship to each other at this stage of the

Key position No. 2

lift. This position is one of the most difficult to pass through for two main reasons:

1. A major weight-arm exists between the active fulcrum of the hips and a vertical line through the bar. The effect of this mechanical disadvantage will be felt especially at this stage.
2. Up to this point the bar has been lifted by vigorous drive of the legs with back remaining in a fixed position.

Now as the legs complete their drive there is an anatomical change-over from one group of muscles to another. The muscles which extend the hip joint will now come strongly into play. Wherever there is such a change-over from one

muscle group to another there will be a weak area. Great determination, therefore, is essential as the lifter passes through this *key position No. 2*.

Maximum Upward Extension

We have already considered the mechanical problems of achieving extension of the body when we were studying the two hands snatch. The same principles are involved for the two hands clean, but remember that because the lifter is handling greater resistance there is a danger that the difficulties encountered can be greater. As the bar passes the knees and the lower part of the thighs the lifter must endeavour to reduce the weight-arm that exists between the active fulcrum of the hips and the weight by forcing the hips in and upwards towards the bar.

Whilst the shoulders will move backwards as a reaction to this movement a conscious effort must be made to keep them forwards over the bar, for as long as possible and especially at the top of the pull. In this way the lifter will maintain himself in an 'upwards lifting position' throughout the movement. Guard most carefully against pulling the shoulders backwards and 'sitting in the chair'. Unfortunately, it is all too easy to fall into this technical error when handling very heavy weights as there is a great desire for the lifter to try to utilise his own body weight against the bar. Coaches must ensure that this does not occur and great care must be taken to ensure that correct technical form is maintained not only in the lifts themselves, but also in all pulling assistance exercises and especially those movements where the weight is lifted either from hang positions or from blocks.

As the lifter forces himself in and towards the bar a second bending of the knees will be observed. This is an anatomical accident but advantage can be taken by a second extension of the knee joint combined with extension of the hips and planter flexion of the ankle joint.

The major joint complexes of ankle, knee and hip lock hard together giving a firm basis for a final elevation of the shoulders at the very top of the

Maximum upward extension: key position No. 3

pull. This complete extension of the body, immediately prior to the lifter dropping into the receiving position, is referred to as *key position No. 3*. The bar bell will have followed the shallow S pathway.

The employment of correct technique will ensure that force has built up thereby developing momentum on the bar. As the lifter moves from the position of maximum extension to the receiving position the bar bell will continue to rise. It is doing so on the momentum that the correctly executed pull has developed. (Remember that as soon as the feet leave the

ground the lifter will be unable to exert force upwards.) At this stage, however, as the feet leave the ground the lifter pulls vigorously on the bar. This action of bending the arm accelerates the lifter's descent under the bar and is an essential aspect of the technique of cleaning.

During this transitional period, or drop, into the receiving position under the bar, the lifter must maintain his trunk in the upright position that he achieved during the pull. All too often lifters fold up by putting their chests down to the bar with the result that the bar slips off the shoulders when they try to receive it.

Receiving Position – Squat Technique

From the position of maximum upward extension the feet are jumped out and to the side and the knees are turned out. This ensures that the hips, whilst travelling slightly backwards from the position they achieved in the extension, may be 'sat down' close between the heels. This ensures that the upper two-thirds of the trunk from the

Receiving position (squat)

From this low position the lifter must recover prior to performing the jerk from the shoulders. This is achieved in the following manner.
Keeping the elbows high the lifter tilts the trunk slightly forwards. This action will lift the buttocks, thereby assisting in the opening of the knee joint which has been under great compression when fully flexed in the low receiving position

umbar spine can be vertical. As the lifter comes into the sitting position the elbows should be brought up and forwards. This position of the elbows fixes the bar bell safely on the top of the chest and shoulder joints. It is held securely on a strong platform of support. Remember also that the elbows must be kept high and clear from the thighs for two sound reasons:
1. Touching the thighs with the elbows during the lift is cause for disqualification.
2. Should the bar bell come forward when the elbows are in contact with the legs there is a strong danger of injury to the wrists.

Squat clean: recovery

and will give those muscles which extend the knee joint a slightly better angle of pull. At the same time he must endeavour to drive strongly upwards. Due to the anatomical action of the *adductor magnus* muscle there is a tendency for the knees to be pulled in towards each other as the lifter rises. This results in the buttocks being thrust backwards and the shoulders dipped further forwards with a consequent danger of dropping the bar. Great effort must be made to keep the knees turned out as the lifter rises to counteract this action. Having stood erect the lifter should step his feet back into hip width position prior to the jerk.

Receiving Position – Split Technique

Whilst the squat technique is taught in most cases, heavy weights can still be lifted employing the split technique. However, the problems inherent in this style, which were explained under the section on the Split Snatch, restrict the lifter from achieving best possible results. However, having reached the position of

Receiving position (split technique)

maximum upward extension the lifter must come off both feet together. The hip action will ensure that he drops down and forwards underneath the bar. He should pull vigorously on the bar bell as his feet leave the floor but must ensure that he maintains the angle of the trunk which will be slightly inclined backwards due to the forward emphasis of the hip movement as he drops under the bar.

Both feet will land at

approximately the same time. The rear foot should be pointing directly fore and aft ar the front foot will have turned slightly inwards with the knee travelling forwards and in the same direction being pushed well forwards over the ankle joint. The hips which must be maintained square to the front will be close to the forward heel. Because of the slight inclination of the trunk backwards, the bar bell can be secured upon the chest withou such a high elbow action as is required in the squat technique. This receiving position requires great sense of balance and when performed correctly is undoubtedly one of the most satisfying and beautiful movements in weight lifting. To recover from this low receiving position the rear leg is stiffened and is used as a rotating prop pivoting on the rear toe. The bar will be tipped slightly backwards thereby helping to relieve pressure on the forward knee, which should be vigorously extended in combination with these two movements. As the front leg nears complete extension the foot is stepped back a few inches. The lifter now pushes off the rear leg which continues to raise the body and bring the weight forwards and upwards, stepping the rear foot into line with the front one to complete this section of the movement prior to the jerk. Before jerking the weight from the shoulders, the lifter may make adjustments of the bar at the neck. This is sometimes necessary as the heavy bar bell presses against the throat and after a hard recovery from the receiving position it is essential that the lifter breathes freely.

Summary of Two Hands Clean

Key Position No. 1 (starting position)

Feet: hip width apart, flat on the floor
Knees: 90–100°
Back: flat but not vertical
Shoulders: slightly in advance of the bar
Head: in comfortable position, eyes looking down about 1½ metres in front of lifter
Hands and arms: hook grip shoulder width, elbows rotated outwards, shoulders brought forwards
This is a dynamic position which the lifter must be in the moment the bar leaves the ground.

Key Position No. 2 (bar at knee height)

Feet: flat on the floor
Shins: vertical
Knees: nearly straight with bar close to the knee cap
Back: flat and having maintained approximately the same angle as at the starting position
Shoulders: in advance of the bar

Arms: straight with elbows rotated out
Head: position maintained
It is essential that the lifter passes through these positions at this crucial stage of the lift.

Key Position No. 3 (maximum upward extension)

Feet: high on toes
Knees: legs and knees straight
Hips: in and up close to the line of the bar bell
Arms: beginning to bend with very strong elevation of the shoulders upwards towards the ears
Head: driving up
By obtaining this key position, momentum will have been passed on to the bar which will continue to rise as the lifter moves his feet.

Key Position No. 4 (receiving position)

SQUAT
Feet: jumped out and apart, flat on the floor
Knees: turned out and pointing over and in same direction as the feet
Hips: will be set back in sitting position but close between the heels

Back: natural curve in the lumbar spine as in sitting position but upper two-thirds of trunk vertical
Arms: the bar bell will be secured high on top of the chest by upward action of the elbows

SPLIT
Feet: split fore and aft, front foot flat on floor with toe turned slightly inwards. Rear foot on ball of foot with heels straight so that the foot is directed to the front
Knees: front knee is bent and pushed forward over the front foot, the rear leg has very slight flexion at the knee joint
Hips: square to the front and close towards front heel
Trunk: inclined slightly backwards due to forward action of the hip joint
Arms: because the trunk is inclined slightly backwards high elbow action is not necessary but the arms are so placed as to secure the bar on top of the chest

The Jerk

Having sufficiently recovered from the clean, the lifter must make certain that he is in a sound, well-balanced position before attempting to drive the bar above his head in the jerk. Often considerable exhausting effort is required in the recovery from the deep squat or the split and the lifter will be breathless. The rules permit him to adjust the weight on the chest.

Having recovered from the clean, the lifter assumes the 'get set' position. This must be well balanced with the weight evenly distributed over the whole of the feet, which are approximately hip width apart. The weight will be resting upon the shoulders on the top of the chest with the elbows pointing forwards and held up. The chest should be lifted and the body straightened out so that the hips are directly under the shoulders. Make certain, also, that the hips are maintained in a position square to the front. The chin should be tucked in so that a clear pathway is permitted for the bar as it is driven close past the face. From this position the lifter

Starting position (jerk)

lowers the body. This is referred to as the dip. Lifters are advised in the early stages to perform this dipping movement slowly and under control. As they become more advanced a faster dipping technique may be employed which will enable the lifter to take advantage of the spring of the bar bell.

Throughout this movement it is essential that the trunk maintains an upright position with the chest high and the elbows up. The depth to which one can lower the body, whilst maintaining this vertical position, is dependent to a great degree upon the flexibility of the ankle joint whilst maintaining the feet flat on the ground. Should the lifter dip too low one of two seriously incorrect positions will be arrived at prior to the upright drive.

1. Maintaining the feet flat on the ground the lifter lowers the body while bending at the knees to a point where the upright trunk can no longer be maintained. In this position the hips move backwards and the trunk is then inclined forwards. This gives a forward direction when the lifter starts to drive against the resistance causing the bar to be thrown forwards of the lifter to a point where it can not be controlled.

2. The lifter maintains the upright trunk position but by dipping too low is compelled to come on to his toes. This causes the knees to move forwards and there is a serious loss of balance as the lifter moves on to a small base. Both these errors reduce the possibility for the completion of the successful lift. As stated earlier, a more advanced lifter can use a faster dip technique. This requires a sudden stop at the appropriate point of the dip.

The dip

The drive

The bar bell will then spring down and up on the lifter's shoulders and by correctly timing the upward spring of the bar the lifter can be greatly assisted in his drive.

From the lowest position of the dip the lifter drives upwards vigorously, still maintaining the vertical position of his trunk, high on to the balls of both feet. This upward drive of the trunk gives impetus to the bar bell and as the bar comes off the chest the arms drive strongly against the bar. At this point, the lifter must split off both feet at exactly the same time, endeavouring to keep the chest

high and aiming to place the upper arms vertically above the shoulder joint as he lands in the high split receiving position. The front foot, in this shallow split, is placed on the floor flat whilst the rear leg travelling backwards lands and pivots on the toe. The split is high so that the forward thigh points upwards towards the lifter. The combined position of front and rear legs act as a buttressing effect whose resultant force is upwards through the body to the bar. Always endeavour to stay high in the receiving position when jerking. If the lifter is forced into a deep split it

Receiving position: Geoff Laws

Receiving position

mobility especially across the front of the hip joint on the side of the rear leg. In order that this may be achieved coaches should consider the possibility of teaching the split jerk first in a weight lifter's technical development.

From the receiving position, the lifter must recover and this is done by tilting the bar very slightly backwards and stepping the front foot in. The bar should then be tilted slightly forwards allowing the rear foot to come into line. In this position the lifter waits for the signal from the referee to replace the bar bell on the platform. It is important to remember that the rules stipulate that both feet must be in line square with the lifter's front. Recovery in the correct technique is most important. Lifters who move the rear foot first cause displacement forwards of the bar bell and frequently lose the weight by dropping it to the front.

Final recovery position awaiting signal from referee to replace the bar on the platform: Newton Burrowes

is unlikely that he will be able to recover. If the rear leg is moved before the front, at the beginning of the split, the hips will be pulled back and the trunk tipped forward. This makes it extremely difficult to support heavy weights above the head as the joints of the shoulders and the hips and the effective centre of the base are not in a line of support.

From the beginning of his training the young lifter must be taught to perform this movement correctly. It is essential that he develops

Summary of the Jerk

Key Position No. 1

Feet: hip width apart, flat on the floor
Trunk: upright, chest held high, hips square to the front and under the shoulders
Arms: elbows held high securing the bar on chest
Head: chin tucked in
In this position the lifter must recover sufficiently from the heavy clean. He should be able to breathe freely. Pause sufficiently to be certain of control in subsequent parts of the movement.

Key Position No. 2 (the dip)

Feet: must remain flat on the floor
Trunk: must maintain its vertical position as in key position No. 1
Elbows: must be kept up supporting the bar on top of the chest
Head: chin tucked in
The success of the lift, to a great degree, will depend on arriving in this position correctly. Make certain that during the dip the elbows do not drop allowing the bar to roll forwards down the chest. The depth to which one can dip, maintaining the upright position of the trunk, will be dependent on the flexibility of the ankle joint whilst maintaining the feet flat on the floor.

Key Position No. 3 (the drive)

Feet: high on toes
Trunk: drives vertically upwards
Arms: beginning to come into play punching vigorously upwards at the top of the drive
Head: driving upwards vertically
This upward drive is an essential and vigorous part of the jerk. It is a movement which can be practised as an assistance exercise. The lifter sometimes fails to take full advantage of this movement, merely dipping and splitting.

Key Position No. 4 (receiving position)

Feet: a short split, front foot flat on floor, rear foot on ball of the toes pointing fore and aft
Trunk: upright, shoulders and hips in a vertical line of support
Arms: strongly locked tight, pressing hard against the resistance
Head: in natural alignment between the arms
Make certain that the split is high, that the body is in correct alignment under the weight and that the head has not been pushed forwards with the hips pulled back. Great determination must be shown in this receiving position. Fight against the bar bell and recover in the prescribed way exercising great control.

Assistance Exercises

For the complete development of our sport it is essential that training is comprehensive. This will mean that in addition to the two Olympic movements of snatch and clean and jerk, assistance exercises must be practised. Broadly speaking these come under two headings.

1. Technical assistance exercises – which are employed initially in the learning process and mastery of technique and are, therefore, an essential part of a beginner's preparation. These also form an important part of an advanced lifter's programming in order that his technical development can be maintained.

2. Other exercises – which can be either technical or general in nature, are employed to develop strength and power and will, therefore, take up a greater proportion of the more advanced lifter's training time. We shall look at specific exercises for each lift in turn.

Power snatch

Two Hands Snatch

Power Snatch
The bar is lifted from the floor to above the head on straight arms with only the slightest bending of the knees. The feet should not be moved. As is clear from the name of this exercise, its objective is to develop power in those muscles employed in the

snatch. Its special value is in compelling the lifter to maintain a long pull.

This exercise can also be performed from various heights as in snatching from the hang, where the bar is held at levels round about the knee, and from blocks of varying height. When the lifter performs these movements, either from the hang or from blocks, it is essential that he is coached most carefully as there is a tendency to try to start the movement by throwing the head and shoulders backwards. This must be counteracted.

Snatch Pulls with Full Body Extension

Here the first phase of the snatching movement, i.e. lifting the bar from the floor to position of full extension, is completed. This exercise can be performed with weights in the following two ranges.

1. Snatch pull to 100 per cent. This means that weights up to the equivalent to the lifter's best performance in the two hands snatch are used. At this range this exercise is highly dynamic.

2. Snatch pulls to maximum. This means that weights are handled that are well above the lifter's snatching ability but that permit the lifter to go through movements which are still essentially those that would be followed in performing the complete lift. It is essential that loss of technique is prevented. These movements are not 'dead lifts.'

In all types of snatch pulls deliberate attempts to bend the arms, as in an upright rowing movement, must be avoided. The lifter must concentrate on strong elevation of the shoulders. Any arm movement is rather as a result of momentum imparted to the bar by the correct build-up of force. Pulling movements for the snatch can be performed from the hang or from blocks but once again it is essential that very careful coaching is given to the lifter performing these movements.

Snatch Balance Exercises

These exercises are used both for teaching the snatch and for the development of power in the receiving position. In addition they help to develop a sense of balance, essential flexibility and confidence to handle heavy weights in the lowest possible receiving positions, which heaviest weights will demand of the lifter.

The first stages of this exercise are essential for learning purposes; they are as follows:

Squat Technique

1. With the feet in the predetermined receiving position the bar is held at arm's length over head. The lifter then squats up and down. This will help him to understand the position required, giving a sense of balance, flexibility and co-ordination.

2. Feet in receiving position. The bar on shoulders behind the neck. The lifter presses the bar to arm's length whilst sinking into the squat receiving position under the bar.

3. Feet in receiving position. The bar on the shoulders behind the neck. The lifter heaves the bar upwards, at the same time dropping into the low receiving position. This is a faster movement, developing the co-ordination of the 'drop'.

4. Feet in the pulling or starting position. Bar on the shoulders behind the neck. The lifter

Snatch balance exercise

heaves the bar upwards at the same time jumping the feet apart to drop into the low receiving position. This completes the co-ordination training for the drop. It is also a movement practised by experienced weight lifters with weights in excess of their best snatching ability. It is then used to develop great power and confidence in the low receiving position. This movement can also be performed with the bar resting on the front of the chest. The objectives of this variation are to teach the lifter how far forward to move his body under the bar to receive it in a position of balance. Again this

is an advanced exercise and heavy weights can be used.

Split Technique

1. Feet in the predetermined receiving position. The bar at arm's length above the head.

The lifter moves up and down in this split position. Again a sense of balance, flexibility and co-ordination will be necessary when he moves under the bar in the complete snatch.

Snatch balance exercise

Split technique snatch balance

2. Feet in the receiving position. The bar on the chest. The lifter presses the bar upwards and slightly forwards to arm's length whilst sinking into the receiving position.

3. Feet in the receiving position. The bar on the front of chest. The lifter heaves the bar up and slightly forwards, dropping into the low receiving position. This is a more dynamic exercise.

4. The front foot drawn slightly back from final receiving position, the bar on front of the chest. With a powerful heave up and slightly forward the lifter steps the front foot into the final receiving position whilst dropping down and low punching the bar to arms length. This latter stage is also performed by the advanced lifter employing split technique with weight in excess of his best snatching ability and is, therefore, an essential power building exercise for the split snatch. Do not perform these movements for the split with the bar bell behind the neck as this tips the trunk forwards. Various stages of these movements are extremely valuable warming-up exercises prior to performing the complete snatch.

Technical/Learning Assistance Exercises for the Snatch

Squat technique

BAR	FEET	ACTION
1. On shoulders behind neck	Receiving position	Press bar and sink into low receiving position
2. On shoulders behind neck	Receiving position	Heave bar and drop into low receiving position
3. On shoulders behind neck	Pulling position	Heave bar, jump feet to receiving position to drop into low receiving position
4. On top of chest	Pulling position	Heave bar, jump feet to receiving position to drop into low receiving position

Split technique

BAR	FEET	ACTION
1. On top of chest	Receiving position	Press bar and sink into low receiving position
2. On top of chest	Receiving position	Heave bar up and slightly forward; drop into low receiving position
3. On top of chest	Front foot slightly drawn back from final receiving position	Heave bar up and slightly forward; drop into low receiving position at the same time stepping front foot into final receiving position

Value
a. Learning the movements
b. Mobility in low positions
c. Balance and confidence in low positions
d. Strength and power in receiving positions,
   e.g. 3 and 4 for squat and 3 for split are very
   important advanced power exercises

Snatch Width Grip Shrugs

This exercise is designed to develop the ability of the lifter to elevate his shoulders strongly at the concluding part of the full extension. It must not be confused with the shoulder rolling movement as employed by body builders. The lifter should use straps whilst performing this movement as the weight must be very heavy. With a snatch width grip the lifter stands erect with the bar resting across the front of the thighs. Keeping the trunk erect and the feet flat on the floor, he bends his knees and then vigorously drives upwards on to his toes, at the same time pulling the shoulders up to the ears. The arms should not bend during this movement. Inclining the trunk forwards during the dip is not recommended as it tends to cause the lifters to pull the shoulders back against the resistance.

Halting Dead Lift

This exercise is similar to snatching from the hang but the position with the bar at knee height is maintained for a period of approximately six

Snatch width grip shrugs

seconds. This places considerable resistance upon the muscles which are employed in the Middle Range of the movement (around key position No. 2), which are working isometrically. At the conclusion of the six-second period the lifter completes the movement reaching up to full extension. The bar is then lowered back to the starting position for this exercise at knee height and the procedure is repeated. It is not necessary to perform many repetitions of this movement as the overload is so great.

Two Hands Clean

Power Clean

The bar is lifted from the floor on to the top of the chest with only the slightest bending of the knees as the bar is received. It is important to remember that the feet must not be moved from the starting position. There is a tendency with heavy weights to try to jump the feet out to the side. This defeats the object of the exercise which is to try to keep the pulling movement going as long as possible thereby developing the muscles responsible for this movement.

The lifter must try, therefore, to maintain as long, and as high, a pull as possible keeping his feet in the initial starting position.

This exercise can be performed from various heights from blocks but it is important that it is carefully coached to avoid any tendency to try to start the movement by leading with the head and shoulders backwards.

Power clean

Clean Pulls with Full Body Extension

This exercise is designed to develop pulling power up to the position of full extension of the body. It is performed with weights in the following two ranges:

1. Clean pull to 100 per cent. Here weights in the range of the lifter's best performance of the two hands clean and jerk are used. The exercise is dynamic and the lifter must concentrate on developing speed within the technical range.

2. Clean pulls to maximum. In these movements the lifter can handle very heavy weights which are above his normal cleaning ability but it must be remembered that correct technique must be maintained in performing these assistance exercises as they are an important part of the complete movement. These movements are not 'dead lifts'.

In all pulling movements for the

Clean pulls

clean deliberate attempts to bend the arms must be avoided. Any arm movement of this nature would prevent correct force being applied to the bar. At the top of the movement the lifter must concentrate on strong elevation of the shoulders. Again these pulling movements can be performed from the hang or from blocks. As the weight is considerable, great care must be taken in the coaching of these movements to ensure that correct technical pathways are maintained.

Clean Grip Shrugs

This exercise throws great resistance upon those muscles which elevate the shoulders and is, therefore, most important in the development of a full and effective extension. Do not confuse this movement with shoulder rolling which is performed by body builders. Using straps and a clean width grip, the lifter stands erect allowing the bar to rest across the front of his thighs. Maintaining his trunk erect and his feet flat on the floor he bends his knees and vigorously drives upwards on to the toes,

Clean grip shrugs

at the same time pulling the shoulders up towards the ears. As this exercise is specific to the muscles which elevate the shoulders, the arms must not be bent during the movement. Be careful not to allow the body to incline forwards to any great degree at the start of the movement as there is a danger that the lifter may try to pull backwards with his shoulders in order to overcome the inertia of the heavy resistance. Remember to drive up strongly.

Halting Dead Lift

This is the same movement as is performed for halting dead

lift for the snatch but now we employ the shoulder width grip. Careful coaching is essential during this exercise.

Whilst all of these exercises listed above will have very definite beneficial effect upon the strength development of the muscles of the legs and hips, there are an additional two specialised leg exercises, depending upon the type of technique employed, which help with recovery from the low receiving position in either split or squat.

1. **Front squats.** The lifter takes the bar on to the front of the chest held in position at the

Front squats

2. Split squats. The lifter takes the bar from the stands on his chest and steps forwards on to a predetermined foot spacing and from this lowers the body down and forwards into the complete split clean receiving position. From here, by stiffening the rear leg, he pushes backwards with the front one and then repeats the movement up and down. This exercise develops great power and mobility in the receiving position and gives great confidence. Do not attempt repetitions of this exercise until you are perfectly balanced. It should be pointed out that strength development is very specific in this movement and often lifters who can produce very good results on the normal back squat will still find considerable difficulty in this movement and be surprised at the initial low poundages that they are able to use.

The Jerk

Jerk Balance

This exercise is valuable both in teaching the jerk from the shoulders to the beginner and

shoulders by the hands. The elbows must be kept up, the feet are placed in position wider than hip width apart with the toes turned out. The lifter now lowers into the deep squat position and from there recovers. This movement is repeated for the specified number of repetitions.
It is essential that the lifter maintains an upright position with the elbows held up throughout the movement. The knees must be kept turned out and apart during the recovery,

fighting against the tendency for the adducter muscles on the inside of the leg to pull the knees in. The feet should be placed in the same position as they will land in during the actual clean. This means that the lifter should perform a squat clean and the position of his feet, when he receives the bar, should then be marked on the platform. It is a good idea to make a permanent painting of this foot spacing in front of the squat stands. The lifter may then step back and place his feet on these marks to perform the exercise.

Split squats

Heave Jerks

This movement is a very valuable power builder. The lifter drives the bar from the chest above the head to arm's length, dipping at the knees and hips to catch the weight. There is no foot movement in this exercise.

for developing power in the receiving position and re-establishing technique for the more advanced lifter. The lifter takes the bar from the stands and taking a very short step forward assumes the starting position in which the weight is evenly distributed over both feet with the trunk nearly vertical. The bar must be resting solidly on the chest and the toe of the rear foot pointing directly fore and aft with the hips set square to the front. From this position the lifter bends both knees quickly and driving upwards vigorously punches the bar above the head with the arms. At the same time the front foot is stepped very slightly forwards and the body is dipped by bending the knee as the bar is received above the head. The lifter then lowers the bar and recovers back to the starting position, withdrawing the front foot slightly.

Jerk from behind Neck

This exercise follows the normal jerking procedure except that the starting position is with the weight on top of the shoulders at the back of the neck.

Jerk balance

Jerk from behind neck

Heave jerks

Quarter Jerks
This exercise is designed specifically to develop power in driving the bar from the chest. It is often performed in racks where very heavy weights can be handled. From the position of the bar resting on the chest the lifter bending the legs and vigorously driving up on to the toes against the resistance. With maximum weights the bar may hardly leave the chest at the top of the drive.

These exercises are technical and can be valuable in the learning process. At the same time they become very important power developers for the more advanced lifters. Listed below are other exercises which whilst being technical in some aspects are generally considered to be more valuable as basic raw power developers.

Power Snatch without Dip
In this exercise the weight is pulled straight to arm's length using a snatch width grip without any bending of the legs at the conclusion of the movements.

Quarter jerks

Isometric Pulls in Racks

Here the lifter exerts maximum force for short periods of time against a bar which may be fixed at any height within racks. The grip may vary from snatch to clean width. These exercises have value in developing muscle groups which may have weaknesses in some areas of their movement.

Pulls to Arm's Length with Dumb-Bells

This is similar to the power snatch movement but heavy dumb-bells are used rather than a bar bell. This requires very much greater control and all-round arm and shoulder power.

Power Cleans with Dumb-Bells

As above.

Supporting Heavy Weights above the Head

Lifters are advised to perform this exercise in racks where safety precautions can be ensured. The exercise is very valuable in developing great determination and courage under the heaviest resistance.

Pulls to arm's length with dumb-bells

Power clean with dumb-bells

Back squats

Jerk with Dumb-Bells
This exercise is performed as for the normal jerk with bar bell.

Heave Jerk with Dumb-Bells
This exercise is performed as for the heave jerk with bar bell.

Back Squats
This exercise is an essential movement in all forms of weight lifting and very considerable resistance can be handled. Weights should be taken from squat stands on to the shoulders behind the lifter's head. From this position he lowers into the full squat position driving up vigorously in recovery.

Squat Jumps

This exercise is especially beneficial in the concluding part of all upward driving movements. The bar bell rests across the lifter's shoulders behind his head and from there he lowers to a shallow squat and, driving high, leaps into the air. In landing the knees are bent to act as shock absorbers. It is important to remember that the lifter must check between each repetition as continuous leaping up and down can have detrimental effects upon the knee joints.

Squat jumps

Leg Press

This requires the use of the leg press machine in which the lifter assumes a position underneath the resistance which is very similar to the starting position were he to be turned on to his feet. The legs are straightened vigorously against the resistance. This develops great power in the first stage of the pull.

Calf Raises

This exercise is specifically for those muscles which assist the lifter to complete the pull by lifting him on to his toes. The exercise is best performed in a special calf-raising machine.

Pressing Movements

There are a variety of types of pressing exercises and a selection from these is essential to the necessary development of arm and shoulder strength. These movements are as follows: military press, seated press, seated inclined press (these movements can be performed by either bar bell or dumb-bells); press behind neck and bench press (for the Olympic lifter bench pressing is regarded as the recuperative exercise to be performed at the end of a schedule to help stimulate relaxed breathing. Very heavy weights should not be used as this tightens up the muscles on the front of the chest and shoulders restricting mobility, thereby making it more difficult for the lifter to hold his arms directly above his head).

Seated press from chest

Press from chest

Starting position: press behind neck

Seated press from behind neck

Good Morning Exercise

This is best performed using a round back technique and is a very important rehabilitative and protective exercise. Lifters are taught correctly to maintain a flat back throughout all lifting movements. Should the resistance, however, be so great that they are strongly pulled into a position where the spine rounds, it is possible for some minor injury to occur to the intrinsic muscles which lie along the spine. The round back good morning exercise is performed to counteract this possible danger. With the bar resting across the back of the neck, feet hip width apart, the lifter unlocks his knees slightly, bends the body forward allowing the spine to curl as he lowers down. He then assumes the upright stance position straightening out the back from this curved position as he stands erect. This means that the muscles which surround the spine are being exercised over their full range of movement. The exercise can be performed with a flat back. There are a number of general weight training exercises which can be of benefit to the Olympic

Round back

lifter. These generally deal with specific muscles groups and may be employed should there be any weakness within one of these groups. Throughout this section we have spoken of the use of straps. In the early stages lifters should perform movements without the use of this aid so that their gripping ability can be developed.

Some of the pulling movements may be performed with the lifter standing on blocks. This is of particular benefit in the development of the initial stages of the pull because the lifter must lower the bar down beyond the normal starting position. Those muscles responsible for the initial start of the lift are compelled to work over a longer range. Generally this exercise may be performed by lifters of advanced qualification only.

Upward jumps with bar bell or dumb-bells in the hands will benefit the driving potential of the lifter throughout the pulling movement. The nature of these types of exercise is very explosive.

Flat back

Exercises for Cardio-Vascular, Circulo-Respiratory Endurance

These general fitness exercises are very important to the weight lifter for the following reason: the overload on the systems in performing the snatch, for example, is not very great, as the duration of the movement is very short; however, it is essential that the lifter has a high level of recovery from one training schedule to the next. Since training programmes are progressive the lifter must have the ability to recover from one bout of heavy work to another quickly.

This type of fitness is developed through running, climbing and swimming activities which last for a considerable length of time: this is achieved by lengthening the work-outs, increasing the number of repetitions in each set and various forms of circuit training.

Wrist and shoulder exercise

Shoulder exercise

Exercises for the Development of Co-ordination, Balance and Dexterity

Many of the technical assistance exercises will help with the development of these qualities. In addition, participation in other sports and games, especially gymnastics and volley ball, will have special beneficial effects. Remember that care must be taken in playing volley ball, basket ball, or hand ball to prevent damage to the fingers or thumbs.

Exercises of a General Nature

The training of a weight lifter is not confined to the use of weights alone. We must consider movements which will assist in the development of speed, flexibility, general cardio-vascular, and circulo-respiratory endurance and activities often associated with other sports which will help to develop co-ordination, balance and dexterity and general awareness of the movement capabilities of the human body.

Exercises for speed may be as follows:

- Performance of power assistance exercises with very light bar bells working at maximum speed
- Sprinting over short distances
- Standing long jump, high jump, and triple jump
- Bounding and leaping movements
- Hurdling
- Hopping
- Leaping up on to objects such as box horse, leaping up flights of stairs etc.
- Shuttle running
- Shadow boxing and skipping

Exercises for Mobility

It is important to note that ballistic movements against the joint do not produce mobility but on the contrary add to the problems of lack of flexibility about the joint being exercised. There are a variety of simple movements which may be performed and the exerciser should relate these to all the major joint complexes, especially ensuring that he is flexible enough to achieve the lowest receiving positions. Those exercises with weights such as the snatch balance movements will greatly assist this essential aspect of a lifter's make-up.

Hamstring mobilisers

Knee and ankle exercises

Trunk rotational

Hamstring mobilisers

Abdominal exercise

Trunk rotational

Chest raises

High jump

Long jump

Summary of Power Assistance Excercises

Technical Exercises

SNATCH	CLEAN	JERK	GENERAL

Power snatch
Snatch balance
Snatch grip pulls
   100 per cent
Snatch grip pull maximum
Snatch grip shrugs
Snatch from blocks
   (various heights; these
   exercises need very
   careful coaching)
Halting dead lift
   (snatch grip)
	Power clean
	Clean grip pulls 100 per cent
	Clean grip pull maximum
	Clean grip shrugs
	Pulls from blocks
	   (various heights; these
	   exercises need very careful
	   coaching)
	Halting dead lift (clean grip)
	Split squats
	Front squats
		Jerk balance
		Jerk from behind neck
		Jerk from racks
		Heave jerks
		Quarter jerks
			Short range power
			   movements for pulls

Raw Exercises

SNATCH	CLEAN	JERK	GENERAL

Power snatch without dip
Isometric pull in racks
Pulls to arm's length with
   dumb-bells
Supporting heavy weights
   above the head
	Power clean without dip
	Power cleans with
	   dumb-bells
	Isometric pulls in racks
		Jerks with dumb-bells
		Heave jerks with
		   dumb-bells
		Supporting heavy
		   weights over head
			Back squats
			Squat jumps
			Calf raises
			Press: military, seated,
			   inclined (bar bell or
			   dumb-bell)
			Round back good morning
			Selected muscle group body
			   building exercises
			Grip development; bench
			   press (light)

Newton Burrowes, British Champion,
jerking 167.5kg

Alexandrov (Bulgaria) jerks 210kg

Training and Preparation Methods

The selection of schedules and training plans has for many years presented the weight lifter with his major training problem. 'How do I train?', 'When do I train?', 'What combination of exercises?', 'Should I concentrate on power-building, technique, fitness training and how are these to be arranged within a training plan?', are questions always in the mind of the athlete. It is hoped that this chapter will help in finding the mainstream of the many varied ideas that exist and will show how by careful attention to the build-up of progressive training methods success can be achieved.

In an involvement in any activity, it is essential that the participant has a philosophy in which he can believe. Such a philosophy must always incorporate the desire to be the best. This quality alone will go a long way in helping to overcome the difficulties and inevitable setbacks that occur in a lifting career. The lifter must understand his sport thoroughly and all the requirements necessary for success. Such knowledge will help to prevent him wasting time on unnecessary activity. He must understand what the term 'fitness' means in relation to his sport and once he has this knowledge he must use it intelligently.

Success breeds success at all levels. Even the greatest champions begin their careers by competing in and winning comparatively minor competitions. These early triumphs are inspirations for further endeavours. They become the buttresses of the individuals' philosophy and are the strengtheners of their determination. Let us consider the philosophy in a little more detail.

Fitness for Weight Lifting

The first consideration can be posed in the question, 'Are you fit to be a successful weight lifter?' Even this question at the outset contains the qualification of success. Anyone can lift weights. Many do so for recreational purposes alone and one must not decry the pleasure that they achieve from such participation. In our context however, success applies to winning – to pushing oneself to the limits of personal ability. What then is our special fitness? The ability to perform the activity of weight lifting with success and to be able to recover quickly. Let us see how this definition can be applied to our sport and what are the essential steps necessary in making it viable.

1. Strength. It is important to develop great strength. This is what the sport is all about. It is the basis. No weak lifters are champions. Fortunately, this is perhaps the easiest aspect of the activity and in our sport the sky is the limit as far as strength development is concerned. Many lifters are much stronger than their technical ability will permit them to show. It is very difficult to give a real definition of strength but basically it is the ability to exert maximum effort for a short period of time without any fast movements being involved. It is in its purest form an isometric activity but for our purposes it would relate to those activities in which movement is considerably limited. We would speak, therefore, of the activity of breaking chains, bending iron bars, very heavy dead lifts as being much closer to pure strength activity.

2. Speed. The quality of speed is the ultimate end product of all major athletic events that are not judged on asthetic presentation or factors of judgement alone. Weight lifting is an explosive activity: maximum force needs to be generated in the shortest possible time. This means that the quicker you can bring into effective play the great strength that you will develop the greater will be your power. It must be pointed out that without great strength, the lifter will not be able to develop speed. Indeed there are no fast-moving weak people.

3. Power. In weight lifting terms power is force (strength) multiplied by velocity (speed). Power is the most important factor in the successful accomplishment of all weight lifting and other athletic events of an explosive nature. Together with strength the quality of speed can be developed and at certain times in the training plan this should be given special attention. In addition to Olympic Weight Lifting, high degrees of power are demonstrated by all athletes involved in short duration activities performed with maximum effort. There are, therefore, many similarities in the athletic requirements of all field events athletes – sprinters, short-distance cyclists and swimmers.

4. Fitness. In preparing a plan and corresponding schedules of work, the lifter often gets carried away by grand ideas of workouts that time proves him to be incapable of completing. The reason why he will be unable to fulfil his best intentions will be his lack of fitness for the work load that he has set himself. Actual physical fitness is very hard to define as it varies considerably from activity to activity. The marathon runner could not be expected to lift the heavy weights handled by the lifter nor the lifter to run the marathon, so the fitness requirements will be seen to be different. In our original definition we talk of being able to recover quickly. This means: having undertaken to train at a certain load level, it is essential that the lifter can recover quickly enough to be able to repeat his training at a similar or greater load level at subsequent training sessions. Often the best laid plans will fail because the lifter cannot recover quickly enough from one workout to another. Strength is developed by resistance overload, general physical fitness is achieved by physiological overload. This simply means that the systems of the body which involve heart, lungs and circulation are stimulated to greater efficiency by subjecting them to levels of work over and above those normally necessary for the ordinary living process. In books on physical education these systems are referred to as cardio-vascular (heart and circulation) and circulo-respiratory (efficient use of oxygen and expiration of carbon dioxide). Since much weight lifting training (training for power) necessitates the use of heavy weights and consequently low repetitions placing heavy overload on the muscular system only, little is done to develop cardio-vascular and circulo-respiratory fitness. The efficiency of these systems in high degree is essential in the work/recovery cycle and, therefore, essential in successful progress planning. In physiological terms much of our training for weight lifting is of an anaerobic nature (muscle work without direct oxygen supply from breathing), but for maximum efficiency work of an aerobic type (with direct oxygen supply from breathing) is also needed. Exercises are described in the previous chapter which have special value in developing fitness.

5. Coaching. In coaching our sport a great deal of attention is always paid to the mastery of the techniques of the lifts, and a sound understanding of the principles of mechanics is essential. In weight lifting the movements of the two lifts are difficult and unusual and it is especially important to remember that they are to be applied to a changing apparatus. By this is meant that there is a considerable difference between a first attempt clean and jerk with a weight that should be overcome comparatively easily, and a third attempt which may well be a personal or even a national or world record. The apparatus has effectively been changed. This change can disturb a lifter psychologically and thereby cause technique to break down. The activity of weight lifting is, therefore, complex. Training schedules must always include work related to the maintenance and development of correct technique. This technique must be reinforced constantly by correct practice of the lifts and the application of technical assistance exercises. At the extreme range of stress, the big championship, your skill must not let you down.

6. Willpower and motivation. At the beginning of this chapter reference was made to the great desire to be the best. The culmination of this desire can be reinforced by many forms of motivational methods. Motivation can be achieved through external rewards such as money, houses, cars, improved job and family prospects and so on, but since such are unlikely to come the way of our athletes, the motivating factors that make the champion must come from within. It is easy to lose heart and if one's philosophy is not balanced, incorporating the basic foundations referred to previously, one's chances of success will be limited. Determination and single-mindedness of purpose are the cornerstones of the strength of character needed by the champion. He must be prepared to work very hard for many years, to overcome the setbacks of injury and defeat. The famous American lifter, Pete George (American and World Champion as a teenager) said 'Anything you want badly enough you can get. Burning desire or enthusiasm is the motivating force that can make a man a champion.' Most people who achieve greatness have innate advantage but it is only by using their natural talents to the full and by working very hard that they reach the top of their chosen field of activity.

Sport is a natural part of man's development. Man is always striving to conquer, to establish himself as the prime living creature. Much progress in the history of mankind has been dependent upon his intelligence, search for knowledge, and its practical application. The development of scientific weight lifting is in its infancy. Consider what the records may be in 100 years time. Man's development in weight lifting, as in other sporting fields, is dependent upon the removal of inhibition.

This is achieved by repeatedly submitting oneself to suitable stressful situations within the training context, and by overcoming them successfully. These conditions exist in both *training* and *competition*. The training plan and schedules must be arranged to overcome such situations. They must be designed to master appropriate stress situations and not create conflicting stress through misapplication or too hasty advancement.

SUMMARY

Our philosophy can be expressed, therefore, in the need for:

- The development of great strength.
- The development of speed and athletic ability.
- The development, consequent on these, of great power.
- The development of systematic fitness and physical hardness.
- The mastery of technique.
- The desire to be the best, reinforced by motivating factors.

The Training Process Analysed

PROBLEMS

One has to choose from many schedules, which may be unscientific or individualistic

Unrealistic appraisal of one's ability in terms of effort and performance

Problems may be either physiological or psychological or both

Other problems internal or external to lifter

ACTS	DANGERS	REQUIREMENTS
Overload on an organ of the body can produce either training or collapse	Overtraining: not enough rest and recovery	Development of great power
Continual progression over long periods without breaks is inconsistent with training process	Undertraining: too much rest means there would be no training of the organ	Development and maintenance of levels of skill
Adequate recovery must follow work for the training process to occur	The schedules of champions must not be copied by reducing weights used	Development of physical fitness related to heavy work loads
The load, volume and intensity require variation and control	Without physiological robustness work load must be low, resulting in little progress	Development of willpower
	Weaknesses must receive attention, training solely on one's strengths is unbalanced training	A desire to be the best: this is best achieved by successful progression
	Mental strain of prolonged competition stress can cause disastrous physiological changes	Detailed personal attention to: Diet: adequate and varied food intake Sleep: sufficient rest/recovery Stress: alleviate undesirable pressures

Training of the Novice Lifter

The twin aims are to acquire *power* and *skill*.

Development of power – This is best achieved by employing those exercises closely related to the classical lifts. These are largely massive and dynamic in nature.

Development of skill – This is best achieved by the repetitive practice of those specially designed assistance exercises aimed at the development of the complete technique.

Stage 1

It is recommended that the novice lifter trains three times a week with each workout followed by a day's rest: e.g. training days 1, 3 and 5 and rest days 2, 4, 6 and 7. The coach has to assess carefully the training weights, emphasising skill rather than heavy weights. Forcing is to be avoided at this stage. Here is a typical example of first stage schedules for a novice lifter.

Training Day 1
Warm-up – running, free-standing exercises, mobility exercises

	sets × reps
Power clean	5 × 5
Snatch balance exercise	5 × 5
Snatch pulls	5 × 5
Back squat	5 × 5

Training Day 2

Warm-up	sets × reps
Power snatch	5 × 3
Jerk balance exercise	5 × 5
Clean pulls	5 × 5
Front or split squats	5 × 5

Training Day 3

Warm-up	sets × reps
Continuous clean and heave press	5 × 5
Snatch balance exercise	5 × 5
Clean – squat or split	5 × 3
Seated dumb-bells press	5 × 5

Schedules should be rounded off with exercises for the trunk: e.g. lower back or abdominals (3 sets × 10 reps). Also included should be exercises for all joint complexes, to maintain and develop full range of mobility, and a short period of light running.

In order that good motor habits be formed the weight of the bar should not be increased for several sessions. When technique has developed and improved small additions can be made gradually. Eventually the ascending bar principle can be introduced.

Stage 2

Progression can now be made to a second stage. An alternate schedules system may be used and can be applied in the following way:
training day 1: schedule A;
training day 3: schedule B;
training day 5: schedule A;
training day 1: schedule B, and so on. The following is an example of such a programme

Schedule A

Warm-up	sets × rep
Snatch	5 ×
High pull	2 ×
	1 ×
Clean grip	2 ×
Jerk balance exercise	5 ×
Front or split	2 ×
Squats	3 ×

Schedule B

Warm-up	sets × rep
Clean and jerk	5 ×
High pull	2 ×
	1 ×
Snatch grip	2 ×
Snatch balance exercise	5 ×
Back squat	5 ×

Schedules should be rounded off with trunk exercises, flexibility exercises for all joint complexes and a short period of jogging. After some six to ten weeks, depending upon the individual's progress, a total should be made in competitive conditions. From the results of this competition his best snatch and clean and jerk will be known. These results will be used by the coach to calculate his future training loads in the ensuing intermediate stage.

Training of Lifters of Intermediate Qualification

Intermediate Stage
The length of the intermediate training plan depends upon the sports calendar, from which the coach selects a particular competition date. The training period can then be fixed but its range is from twelve to fifteen weeks. This period should then be divided into the following phases:
1. Preparatory period
2. Competitive period
Assuming a 14-week build-up prior to the selected competition, training will be divided into three blocks: weeks 1–4, weeks 5–8 and weeks 9–14.

Preparatory period (weeks 1–4). The lifter now trains four times a week. Special attention should be paid to the development of fitness, including specialised strengthening and technique. Whilst the tonnage will be high, the intensity will be low. The training/recovery cycle is managed by alternating heavy and light training weeks. Thus week 1 is a light week, week 2 heavy, week 3 light, week 4 heavy. However, there is a definite progression, for example in week 4 the lifter is aiming to get a best ever for 5 reps on most lifts. In the case of a lifter whose best snatch is 60 kgs, he would start week 1 with a top set for 5 reps at about 70 per cent, i.e. 42½ kgs, week 2 at 47½ kgs, week 3 down to 45 kgs, and week 4 up to 50 kgs, (approx. 80 per cent) hopefully for a new best for 5 reps. During weeks 1–4 all exercises will be done as 5 sets of 5 reps (with the exception of hyperextensions and abdominal exercises which will be done 3 × 10 throughout). All sets are done with progressively heavier weights until the last set which is a 'drop down' set, i.e. the heaviest set is always the last but one.
An example of a schedule that might be applied in the preparatory period is as follows. (N.B. The exercises listed are only suggestions and the coach may vary these according to his assessment of the lifter's strengths and weaknesses. Also, the order of the exercises may be changed: e.g. some lifters prefer to use squat assistance exercises before pulling assistance exercises, or if a lifter is a weak jerker, he may put this exercise first in his schedule.)

Schedule for weeks 1–4:

Day 1	Day 2	Day 3	Day 4
Snatch	Snatch balance (behind neck or split)	Snatch balance (behind neck or split)	Clean
Power clean	Snatch pulls	Power clean	Power snatch
Clean pulls	Front/split squats	Clean pulls	Snatch pull
Jerk from racks	Dumb-bell press	Jerk from racks	Front/split squats
Back squat	Hyperextensions	Back squat	Press behind neck
Sit-ups		Sit-ups	Hyperextensions

In a normal week on the above schedule it is suggested that ideally the lifter trains two days, rests one, trains two, rests two. However, this may not be possible for all (see appendix for variations of this).

Competitive period (weeks 5–14). During weeks 5–9 the lifter uses 2 × 5 and 5 × 3 for all exercises, excepting abdominals and hyperextensions. The schedules below are suggested, subject to coaches' variations.

During weeks 10–13 the lifter uses 6 × 3 for his pulls. Squats should be done 3 × 5 followed by 3 × 3. Week 10 is light (70–75 per cent of best lifts). Week 11 is medium (85 per cent of best lifts). Week 12 is heavy (90 per cent of best lifts for the top set, plus 5 or so singles of 100 per cent). During week 13 the lifter trains up to starting weights or 10 kgs below. Week 14 is a tapering-off week: workouts should only last between 45 minutes and 1 hour so that energy reserves are built up. During these final weeks the lifter should get sufficient sleep, adequate nutrition and practise good living habits. The schedules set out for weeks 5–9 will be continued until the end of week 12 but with changes in sets and reps for each exercise as shown on the next page.

Then schedule for weeks 5–9:

Day 1	Day 2	Day 3	Day 4
Snatch	Clean and jerk	Snatch	Clean and jerk
Power cleans	Snatch balance	Power clean	Snatch balance
Clean pulls	Snatch pulls	Clean pulls	Snatch pulls
Jerk from rack	Back squat	Push press (behind neck)	Press behind neck
Front/split squats	Hyperextensions	Front/split squats	Hyperextensions
Sit-ups		Sit-ups	

	Week 10:	Week 11:	Week 12:
	Light week	*Medium week*	*Heavy week*
Snatch, and clean and jerk	5 × 3	2 × 3 5 × 2	2 × 3 2 × 2 5 singles
Snatch balance	5 × 3	2 × 3 3 × 2	1 × 3 2 × 2 3 singles
Press behind neck	2 × 5 3 × 3	2 × 5 3 × 3	2 × 5 3 × 3
Power snatch; power clean; push press behind neck	5 × 3	3 × 3 3 × 2	3 × 3 3 × 2

During week 13 the following schedule is used:

Monday	*Tuesday*	*Thursday*	*Friday*
Snatch	Clean and jerk	Power snatch	Snatch
Snatch pulls	Clean pulls	Power clean	Clean and jerk
Front/split squats	Back squats	Front/split squats	
Hyperextensions	Hyperextensions		

All exercises with the exception of pulls should be 3 × 3, then 5 singles working up on the lifts to intended starting poundage or at least 10 kgs below. Pulls should be 3 × 3 followed by 5 × 2. The final week is an effective tapering-off up to the competition day. Gains in strength can hardly be expected during this period and all lifts should form a pattern of 'successful rehearsal', building confidence and a positive approach towards the forthcoming competition. Rest and relaxation are important requirements. Daily body weight checks should be made. The importance of the day of the competition demands that the lifter should not be distracted. He should check all personal kit, arrive early at the weigh-in, and ensure he has access to high energy foods which are easily digested. Lifters who have successfully completed the novice and intermediate training programmes will now be suitably prepared for more rigorous loads and plans as employed by lifters of advanced qualification.

Training of Lifters of Advanced Qualification

As one of the principle aims of training is to show continuously improving results, it is essential that those qualities of which we have already spoken should be fully developed. This will take time, possibly many years, and bearing this in mind it is essential that planning be undertaken by the coach or lifter to this end.

Planning falls into two categories, those of a long-term nature and those of short-term. Short-term plans will be 'run ups' to major competitions and as such are a part of the long-term plan. Within the plan, detailed realistic analysis of all goals to be achieved must be considered. This involves consideration of the sports calendar and preparation of individual sessions, organisation of the week's training, month and month group cycles; these together make up the final plan whether it be for a unit of 6, 9 or 12 months. These cycles, within the plan, will have different emphasis according to the relationship, timewise, to

principal competitions, and may be selected for the development of skill and technique, power building, fitness etc.

Group planning can be employed but for most advanced lifters plans are individually prepared. Such plans will, however, have the same ingredients as those for the group but it will be likely that additional technical work, supplementary exercises and varied overload and volume will be included. Generally speaking, the advanced lifter should train all the year round and this training can be broken down into two main cycles planned for two major competitions. There should be intermediate competitions, as results in these will be used in determining the load for the forthcoming cycle. They will also help to show up weaknesses both technical and also in the previously completed training cycle. Lifters should compete five or six times per year with two of these being competitions in which it is hoped to achieve the highest results; but at intermediate competitions the lifter should still aim for

personal 'bests' as these will be the essential steps of progress and confidence reinforcement. Each major competition for which we plan must have a training cycle based on the following periods: preparatory, competitive and transitional.

1. Preparatory period. The length of this period will depend upon the qualification of the lifter, indeed for those in the novice category all their training may be considered under this heading. Much consideration should be given to the development of fitness, speed, co-ordination and endurance in the early stages. The advanced lifter spends most of his time on the assistance exercises with time devoted to the classical lifts being small. Towards the end of this period however more attention will be spent on the snatch and clean and jerk.

2. Competitive period. During the competitive period greater attention is paid to the classical lifts and those assistance exercises closely related to them. Maximum weights, within the range 90 per cent to 100 per cent, are used more frequently and certain exercises are advanced to the

110 per cent + range. During the last 30 to 20 days before competition those exercises which are slow and use maximum weights are generally reduced or excluded. The emphasis should be placed on power, so weights in the region of 90 per cent + are best used. Only a few of the most advanced lifters apply maximums in pulls and squats during the last 14 to 7 days and then with some five or six single reps only. During this period energy expenditure should not be high.

3. Transitional period. The transitional period is in fact a link between the competitive and a new preparatory period to follow and should provide the lifter with a period of active rest. It should be arranged so that whilst the volume and intensity of the load is decreased and the number of training sessions in the week's cycle is cut down, the essential high levels of physical fitness are maintained and improved. This period can last up to four weeks.

It is essential to remember in all planning that the organism cannot maintain a steady high level for a long period and its efficiency tends to rise and fall. This must be taken into consideration when preparing all work cycles and the volume and intensity of the load must be varied providing weeks of maximum, large, medium and light load and indeed within each week similar loading for each training session (see charts for variations in the daily and weekly cycles). Many of those lifters who enjoy ideal training conditions are able to train twice a day, morning and afternoon. Their work load is very high and they are placed in situations of great physical stress. Such people have very high levels of physical fitness and recuperative powers and their tolerance of the stressful situation is very well developed. Such work requires careful medical supervision at all stages.

The following example is a long-term plan which could be followed by lifters of the highest qualification. It gives a build-up to two major competitions. These build-ups will last over a period of 12 weeks including preparatory and competition phases and will lead up to the first competition. This will be followed by a short rest period and then a second 12-week build-up will begin. This spacing of training programmes is usual as success in one competition will mean the lifter being selected for competitions at higher levels and so the plan must aim to 'peak' to achieve the highest possible results.

Training Programme for National Squad Lifters

The first 12 weeks will be split up into three blocks, weeks 1–4, weeks 5–10, and weeks 11–12. During weeks 1–4 and 5–10 the same basic schedule will be followed but during weeks 1–4 all exercises will be done 5 sets x 5 reps (with the exception of hyperextensions which will be 3 sets x 10 reps throughout). During weeks 5–10 all exercises are done 3 sets x 5 reps, then 5 sets x 3 reps, hyperextensions excluded. All exercises are done with a progressively heavier weight until the last set which is a 'drop down set'; that is, the heaviest set is always the last but one.

A system of heavy and light weeks is used alternately, i.e.

week 1 is a light week, week 2 a heavy week, week 3 light, week 4 heavy and so on. However, there is a definite progression, for example in week 4 the lifter is aiming to get a best ever for 5 reps on most lifts. Let us consider the snatch, and say that the lifter's record for a single is 100 k. He would start week 1 with a top set for 5 reps at about 70 per cent, i.e. 70 k; week 2 it is up to 75 k, week 3 down to 72.5 k and then week 4 up to 80 k (approx. 80 per cent) for a new best for 5.

This progression of heavy and light weeks carries on for weeks 5–10 but the reps change, as mentioned, and 3-rep bests are worked on, aiming for about 90 per cent for 3 in week 9.
It is considered that for national-calibre lifters four workouts per week are the absolute minimum for progress and five is better. (Some lifters will work six). With this in mind two separate schedules have been worked out to cater for lifters who train four times per week or five

times per week.
The exercises listed are only suggestions and others may be put in at the discretion of the lifter and his coach, for instance to cater for individual weaknesses. Also the order of the exercises may be changed, e.g. if a lifter is a weak jerker he may put this exercise first, etc.

Lifter Who Trains 4 Times per Week

Day 1	Day 2	Day 3	Day 4
Snatch	1. Snatch balance (behind neck or split)	1. Snatch balance (in front or split)	1. Clean
Power clean	2. Power snatch	2. Power clean	2. Power snatch
Clean pulls	3. Snatch pull	3. Clean pull	3. Snatch pull
Jerk from rack	4. Front squat (split squat)	4. Jerk from rack	4. Front squat (lunge split squat)
Back squat	5. Press behind neck	5. Back squat	5. Press behind neck
	6. Hyperextensions		6. Hyperextensions

In a normal week on this schedule it is suggested that ideally the lifter train two days rest one, train two rest two. However this may not be possible for all.

Lifter Who Trains 5 Times per Week

Day 1	Day 2	Day 3	Day 4	Day 5
1. Snatch balance (behind neck or split)	1. Power clean	1. Snatch	1. Snatch balance (in front or split)	1. Power clean
2. Power snatch	2. Clean pull	2. Clean	2. Power snatch	2. Clean pull
3. Snatch pull	3. Jerk from rack	3. Snatch pulls	3. Snatch pull	3. Jerk from rack
4. Front squat (lunge)	4. Back squat	4. Clean pulls	4. Front squat (lunge)	4. Back squat
5. Press behind neck	5. Hyperextensions		5. Press behind neck	5. Hyperextensions

It is suggested that the lifter train three days in a row rest one, train two, rest one. After this ten-week programme the last two weeks prior to the first major competition should go as follows: all exercises with the exception of pulls should be 3 sets of 3 reps, then 5 sets of 1 rep, working up in the lifts to intended starting attempts or at least 10 k below. Pulls should be 3 sets 3 reps followed by 5 sets 2 reps.

Week 11

Monday	Tuesday	Thursday	Friday
1. Snatch	1. Clean and jerk	1. Power snatch	1. Snatch
2. Snatch pull	2. Clean pull	2. Power clean	2. Clean and jerk
3. Front squat lunge	3. Back squat	3. Squat lunge	
4. Hyperextension	4. Hyperextension		

Week 12

Monday and Tuesday as week 11	Wednesday
	1. Power snatch: 3×3 plus 3×2
	2. Power clean and jerk: 3×3 plus 3×2

Following the first major competition several days of active rest' followed by light training are advised. For the following nine weeks a programme of three weekly cycles of light, medium and heavy weeks begins. As far as exercises are concerned, the lifter trains on the original 4/5 days per week programme he used in weeks 1–10 prior to the first competition. He will now substitute an extra snatch and clean exercise instead of power clean and power snatch, i.e. he will clean and snatch twice a week and power snatch and power clean once a week. He should clean *and* jerk in one of these.

All pulls should now be done 8 sets of 3 reps. Squats should be done 3 sets of 5 reps followed by 5 sets of 3 reps. The breakdown of sets and reps for the light, medium and heavy weeks is as follows for all other exercises:

	light	medium	heavy
	sets × reps	sets × reps	sets × reps
Snatch and clean and jerk	5 × 3	2 × 3	2 × 3
		8 × 2	2 × 2
			8 × 1
Snatch and balance	5 × 3	5 × 3	5 × 3
Press behind neck	3 × 5	3 × 5	3 × 5
	3 × 3	3 × 3	3 × 3
Power snatch and Power clean	5 × 3	3 × 3	3 × 3
		3 × 2	3 × 2

At the end of the ninth week, i.e. after three cycles as suggested above, the lifter uses the same programme as he did for the two weeks prior to the first competition.

Following the second competition, lifters should take two or three weeks of 'active rest' from lifting. This, however, does not mean no training. On the contrary, this time should be spent on fitness training where the lifter will try to increase his cardio-vascular respiratory fitness. The type of work done will depend on the equipment and facilities available but it must be of a progressive nature, e.g. repetition 60-metre sprints, circuit training, non-body contact ball games etc.

Workouts should be recorded in the normal way.

Following this period, which may include some general weight training toward the end, another programme similar to the previous build-up will be planned with a view to producing totals in subsequent important competitions. Lifters should not be afraid to compete during various stages of their programme in matches and these should be treated as gauges of progress in the production of the desired totals at the major matches. Training records must be kept at all times in a notebook.

Page 102 shows a short-term programme over a period of ten weeks to competition. It is based upon a 4-week preparation period and a 6-week competitive period and would be a suitable programme for the experienced lifter building up over a short period of time to a major competition.

The first four weeks of this programme lay down a high level of fitness based upon exercises following the principle of 5 sets of 5 repetitions, then within the range of 70–80 per cent of the best effective achievement for each exercise. This follows a period of four weeks within the competitive phase in which the lifter builds up to best results for the various exercises. The subsequent two weeks lead the lifter in a tapering-off period to the day of the competition. The programme is prepared for lifters able to work on five sessions per week. Arrangements for the workouts will depend upon availability of facilities but with the exception of the last two weeks it is suggested that a rest day between sessions 3 and 4 may be of benefit to the lifter,

allowing him to recuperate. An alternative plan for the final week should involve rest on day 3 with day 4 to include the power snatch and power clean and jerking exercises. Some lifters prefer this, finding two days' rest before a competition too long out of contact with the bar, but the lifter will be able to make up his own mind as to which is most beneficial in his final preparation.

Short-Term Training Cycles

The following charts show variations in training loads over short periods and their arrangements day by day.
Diagram A. In this programme a balance between rest and activity is achieved by alternate day training. The load of the workouts varies and shows that there are heavy loadings on days 3 and 5. Subsequent heavy loadings would not be undertaken until days 11 and 13.

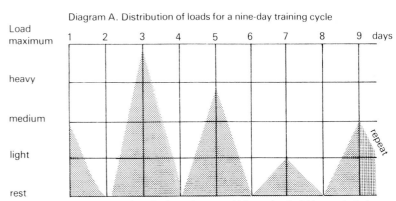

Diagram A. Distribution of loads for a nine-day training cycle

This plan provides for 1 maximum and 1 heavy load within a period of nine training days (novice qualification)

Date		Week 1	Week 2	Week 3	Week 4	Week 5	Week 6	Week 7	Week 8	Week 9	Week 10
		All exercises 5 sets of 5 reps after warm-up at % of best for each exercise				3 × 5 and 5 × 3	5 × 3 and 5 single attempts	3 × 5 and 5 × 3	5 × 3 and 5 single attempts	Olympic lifts to starter or 10 kgs below	Very light
DAY 1	Snatch balance Power snatch Snatch pull Front or split squats Press behind neck	70%	75%	72.5%	80%	Top set 80%	Top set 85% Singles to 95%	Top set 80%	Top set 90% Singles to 100% or New best	Snatch 3 × 3 5 × 1 Snatch pull 3 × 3 5 × 2 Front split squats 3 × 3 5 × 1 Hyperextensions	To starter 5 × 2 5 × 1
DAY 2	Power clean Clean pull Jerk from rack Back squat Hyperextensions	,,	,,	,,	,,	,,	,,	,,	,,	Clean and jerk 3 × 3 5 × 1 Clean pull 3 × 3 5 × 2 Back squats 3 × 3 5 × 1 Hyperextensions	To starter 5 × 2 5 × 1
DAY 3	Snatch Clean Snatch pull Clean pull Abdominals	,,	,,	,,	,,	,,	,,	,,	,,	Rest	Power snatch 3 × 3 3 × 2 Power clean and jerk 3 × 3 3 × 2
DAY 4	As day 1	,,	,,	,,	,,	,,	,,	,,	,,	Power snatch 3 × 3 5 × 1 Power clean 3 × 3 5 × 1 Front/split squats 3 × 3 5 × 1	Rest
DAY 5	As day 2	,,	,,	,,	,,	,,	,,	,,	,,	Snatch 3 × 3 5 × 1 Clean and jerk 3 × 3 5 × 1	Rest
COMPETITION DAY											Championship

Diagram B. This shows a great physiological overload as additional maximum loading is included in day 10 of the programme.

Diagram C. This programme includes a second heavy loading within a period of 9 days. Following from the previous programme (diagram B) the overload principle has been increased by again shortening the period of maximum loading so that there are now two maximums within a period of 9 days.

Diagram D. The final diagram illustrates a programme which involves the principle of stress day training. This is indicated as day 5 and it will be noted that this is a 'maximum plus' training day. Stress day training can only be included in the programmes of the most advanced lifters who have extremely high levels of recovery fitness. The stress is placed upon the lifter by programming lifts which must be attempted which equal or are greater than previous best attempts. This means that the lifter develops determination and courage to a very high degree and is constantly pressurising himself to handle

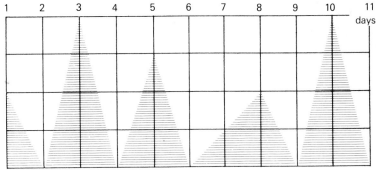

Diagram B. Distribution of loads for a ten-day training cycle

This plan provides for 2 maximum and 1 heavy loads within a period of ten training days (intermediate qualification)

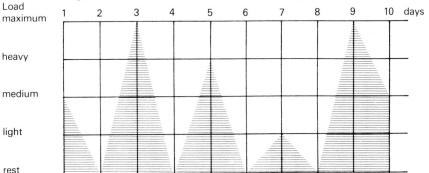

Diagram C. Distribution of loads for a nine-day training cycle

This plan provides for 2 maximum and 1 heavy loads within a period of nine training days (1st class qualification)

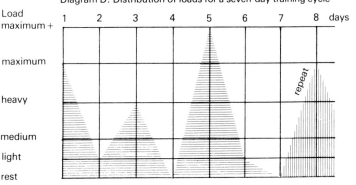

Diagram D. Distribution of loads for a seven-day training cycle

This plan provides for 1 maximum + , 1 maximum, 1 heavy load within a period of seven training days (advanced qualification)

very heavy weights which will in turn affect the level of general training weights in daily schedules and subsequent short-term training plans. Because this type of training demands the expenditure of great amounts of nervous energy it can only be recommended for those lifters who have followed training programmes which have developed very high levels of 'weight lifting recovery efficiency'.

Breakdown of the Last Month's Training Cycle Prior to Competition

Often the last few weeks prior to the competition create the greatest problems to the lifter in organising his final preparation. It is essential that the lifter peaks to achieve the best possible result to the day. Often lifters achieve their best results before the competition or after it. This indicates that the training programme has not been properly organised. There are two different approaches that can be adopted depending upon the qualification of the lifter. Those lifters of first-class or

intermediate qualifications can lift heavier weights closer to the competition day. This is possible for several reasons including the fact that although the weights may be the personal best of the lower standard lifter the weights, in weight lifting terms, are still comparatively light and do not place so great a stress, both psychological and physiological, upon the lifter. In this way the heaviest weights can be lifted in the week immediately prior to the week of competition. This is not the case, however, for the lifters of the highest qualification, and

the greatest weights should not be attempted in the last two weeks prior to the day of competition. From this period some twenty days before the competition, the lifter tapers off, especially in the quantity of work that he is doing, in order that he may build up reserves of energy and enthusiasm and determination.

The diagram shows how this last monthly period can be arranged for lifters of different qualifications. Note that it is very important that a success pattern should be developed and that there should be no failures during this time.

	Week 1	Week 2	Week 3	Week 4						
				Days						
				1	2	3	4	5	6	7
For lifters of 1st class and intermediate qualification	Light volume	Medium volume	Heavy intensity (low reps, heavy weights)	Medium heavy intensity 1 ¼ hrs only	Rest	Very light 5kg below first attempt	Rest	Rest	Competition	
For lifters of advanced qualification	Medium volume	Heavy intensity (top set 90%, singles 100% +)	Olympic lifts to first attempts (Singles: 10kg below best result)							
	Build-up period. There should be no failure during this time.			Final week						

20-Week training cycle

This chart illustrates a build-up of training volume through a preparatory phase of fourteen weeks tapering down through a competitive phase of six weeks. The programme illustrates a build-up of varying volumes of work, week by week. This works on the principle that each week requires a different type of loading and so the training is based upon the principles of building up, cutting back and building up again. Since it is not possible to maintain a continuous week-by-week build-up this cutting-back principle is essential to allow a certain amount of recovery between each weekly cycle. This 20-week period is applicable to lifters of advanced grade only but similar programming can be arranged over 10- or 12-week programmes.
In the 10-week programme the preparatory period would last for six weeks and the competitive for four weeks; and in the 12-week programme the preparatory period would last for eight weeks and the competitive for four weeks.

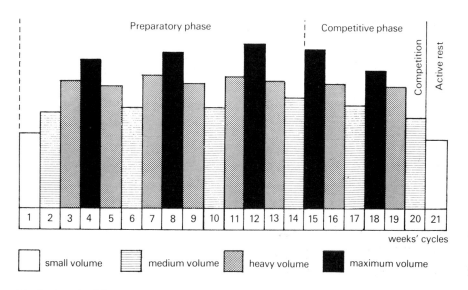

Distribution of training volume on a weekly basis in the preparatory and competitive phases of a 20-week cycle (for lifters of advanced grade)

Where periods of 'active rest' are indicated this refers to a change in the nature of the training programme. For instance, such a period may exclude the use of weights altogether and may concentrate on games, swimming and other relaxing activity. This is especially valuable in the recuperation of the psychological problems created by intensity of competition. This will permit the lifter to tackle the next build-up with enthusiasm and renewed determination.

Rules

International Rules for Snatch and Clean and Jerk

1. Two hands snatch

The bar bell shall be placed horizontally in front of the lifter's legs. It shall be gripped, palms downwards, and pulled in a single movement from the ground to the full extent of both arms above the head, while either 'splitting' or bending the legs. The bar shall pass with a continuous movement along the body of which no part other than the feet may touch the ground during the execution of the lift. The weight which has been lifted, must be maintained in the final motionless position, the arms and legs extended, the feet on the same line, until the referee's signal to replace the bar on the platform. The turning over of the wrists must not take place until the bar has passed the top of the lifter's head. The lifter may recover in his own time, either from a 'split' or a 'squat'.

The referee's signal shall be given as soon as the lifter becomes absolutely motionless in all parts of the body and has his feet and bar bell in line and parallel to the plane of the trunk.

Incorrect movements
1. Pulling from the hang.
2. Pause during the lifting of the bar.
3. Uneven extension of the arms.
4. Incomplete extension of the arms.
5. Finishing with a 'press-out'.
6. Bending and extending the arms during the recovery.
7. Touching the ground with the knee or buttocks or any part of the body other than the feet.
8. Leaving the platform during the execution of the lift if he touches with any part of a foot, the floor outside the limits of the platform.
9. Replacing the bar on the platform before the referee's signal.
10. Dropping the bar after the referee's signal to replace the bar.
11. Failing to finish with the feet and the bar bell in line and parallel to the plane of the trunk.

2. Two hands clean and jerk

1st part: the clean

The bar shall be placed horizontally in front of the lifter's legs. It shall be gripped, palms downwards, and brought in a single movement from the ground to the shoulders, while either 'splitting' or bending the legs. The bar must not touch the chest before the final position. It shall then rest on the clavicles, or on the chest above the nipples, or on the arms fully bent. The feet shall be returned to the same line, legs straight, before performing the jerk. The lifter may make this recovery in his own time.

2nd part: the jerk

Bend the legs and extend them as well as the arms so as to bring the bar to the full stretch of the arms vertically extended. Return the feet to the same line, arms and legs extended and await the referee's signal to replace the bar on the platform. The referee's signal shall be given as soon as the lifter becomes absolutely motionless in all parts of the body and has his feet and the bar bell on the same line, parallel to the plane of his trunk. Important remark – after the clean and before the jerk, the lifter may assure the position of the bar. This must not lead to confusion. It cannot mean in any case, granting a second movement to the lifter, but of allowing him:

(a) Either to withdraw his thumbs or to 'unhook' if he has used this method;

(b) or if the bar is placed too high and impedes his breathing or causes a pain, to lower it in order to rest it on his shoulders;

(c) or to change the width of his grip.

Incorrect movements – clean

1. Any unfinished attempt at pulling in which the bar has reached at least the height of the knees.

2. Pulling from the 'hang'.

3. Cleaning in two or more movements.

4. Touching the ground with the knee or buttocks or any part of the body other than the feet.

5. Any clean in which the bar touches a part of the trunk before the final position at the shoulders.

6. Cleaning in the 'squat' position, touching the knees or thighs with the elbows or arms.

7. Leaving the platform during the execution of the lift, if he touches with any part of a foot, the floor outside the limits of the platform.

Incorrect movements – jerk

8. Any apparent effort of jerking which is not completed.

9. Uneven extension of the arms.

10. Pause during the extension of the arms and finishing with a 'press-out'.

11. Bending and extending the arms during the recovery.

12. Leaving the platform during the execution of the lift, if he touches with any part of a foot, the floor outside the limits of the platform.

13. Replacing the bar on the platform before the referee's signal.

14. Dropping the bar after the referee's signal to replace the bar.

15. Failing to finish with the feet and the bar bell in line and parallel to the plane of the trunk.

Safety

Weight Lifting Safety for Teachers and Coaches

Every teacher wants to prevent accidents in physical education. Accident victims may suffer physical and psychological injury and distress with impaired future happiness. The P.E. programme may be cut back and all sorts of restrictions introduced. Teachers, coaches and authorities may also suffer stress and loss by being sued for negligence and damages if students are injured while using defective equipment; if there was inadequate supervision; if reasonable care was not exercised by the teacher.

To protect your pupils, your employers, your programme, your budget, yourself, give full consideration to the recommendations set out below:

General Physical Education

1. Have all equipment inspected regularly. Report in writing all deficiencies in apparatus, mats, floor surfaces, rigs, equipment, etc. to your superior. Don't use until put right. Get the best equipment and keep in good condition.

2. Make sure you have taught all the necessary skills, including safety procedures, before requiring students to exercise them in game, class or competition situations.

3. Get medical approval before putting an injured student back into game, class or competition activity. Get and follow medical advice.

4. Beginners need special teaching and supervision. A champion trying out an entirely new skill is a beginner at that skill. Supervision means being there when needed.

5. Fatigue often precedes accidents. Students must be fit, at the time, for the work to be attempted. A tired pupil is often accident-prone.

Weight Training and Lifting

In addition to the above, also keep the apparatus locked up unless at least three people want to use it.

1. Ensure that your layout for the different exercises in the weight training area is carefully planned. Bar bells should not be too close to each other. Use mats under the weights. Transport of equipment requires great care. Do not permit horseplay.

2. Check the bar bells, stands, benches, dumb-bells etc.,

carefully before use. Make sure all collars are tight and bar bells evenly loaded. Check each time apparatus comes out and after every set. Your responsibility.

3. Only train in an area where the floor is even, firm and non-slip. Do not permit pupils to train in bare feet. Balance in progressive resistance training is very important.

4. Check and service your equipment regularly. It's good insurance.

5. Know why and when to teach specific exercises as well as how. Good intentions are no excuse for ignorance. Attend an official coaching course.

6. Make sure that stand-ins (two) are used for all exercises, one each side of the bar bell ready to assist. Teach all pupils how to stand-in and catch. See stand-in knows when and how to help.

7. Ensure that pupil does not attempt limit poundages too soon. Too great a weight = bad body position = accident.

8. Teach exercises carefully. Ensure strict exercise principles are employed at all times. Every pupil must advance at his own level.

9. Use only token resistance during exercise learning phase.

When muscle groups are weak they lack control. Lack of muscular control can lead to injury. Proceed with caution and always with careful supervision.

10. Correct breathing on all lifts must be taught. Apply correct training principles.

11. Encourage the use of warm clothing to train in and fast training procedure to avoid 'local chilling' of muscles. Employ correct training principles.

12. Before driving your pupils to advanced training schedules or too early competitions, get your motives clear. Unless the well-being and safety of the performers comes above personal vanity and ambition it could be a dangerous programme. Integrity.

13. Display these recommendations in the gymnasium and ensure all students are familiar with the recommendations. Have your rules and enforce them. Stay in charge.

Weight Lifting Safety for Pupils and Competitors

The use of weights as a means of developing strength and power is very old indeed. Weight training, i.e. strength and muscle building, is a very worthwhile end in itself. Strength is respectable. It assists in the development of skill acquisition and is an important aspect of any physical fitness programme. The sport of weight lifting is exciting, requiring great strength, speed, mental control, fitness and courage and mastery of technique. Many of the world's greatest athletes employ progressive resistance principles in their training.

Weights, however, are impartial apparatus, they make no distinction between beginners or champions. Their use requires careful thought. The skills of the activity must be learnt very carefully. Poor technique, reckless advancement of poundages, irresponsible behaviour, can cause accidents. Listen to your coach or teacher. Apply the correct training principles, respect the limitations of each individual. Get your thinking right. Do it before you start to train.

People say some unkind things about athletes who do not think and so get hurt. 'Don't worry he is all muscle, especially the head' . . . 'He is as strong as an ox, and almost as clever' . . . 'That was lucky Joe, you'd have been in real trouble if you'd landed anywhere other than on your head'. Of course an injury may result from somebody else not thinking but if you think and behave responsibly you will never hurt yourself or anybody else. Consider the following . . .

1. Confidence should not be confused with recklessness; the former is built on knowledge, the latter on ignorance. The only impression reckless weight training makes is on the floor.

2. Although weight training and weight lifting are great fun because you can see and take pride in the progress you are making, to become an expert still takes time – time spent on understanding and mastering each step before moving on to the next. Don't try to run before you can walk.

3. Before trying the next exercise or training plans and schedules get and follow advice from your teacher or coach. The teacher's or coach's job is to ensure that all the experiences you will have from the use of weights will be pleasant ones.

4. Never train alone, always have one stand-in at each end of the bar. Stand-ins should know what you are going to do and when.

5. Keep to your schedule of exercises. Do not advance to poundages without your coach's advice. Do not sacrifice correct body position for poundage.

6. Do not try to keep up with others who may seem to be making more rapid progress than yourself. Train at your own level and within your own capabilities. You will make progress.

7. Horseplay and practical jokes can be very dangerous. If you are not getting enough fun out of serious weight lifting work, it's a poor programme. Wear firm training shoes and warm clothing.

8. Check all apparatus before use and after each exercise. Check collars. Make sure they are firmly secured. Make sure

all bars are evenly loaded. Concentrate and be safety conscious.

9. When you are ready for competition lifting it will require that you have followed a sound training programme. Technique must be mastered. Strength and power building must be developed steadily. Your success in competition will depend upon a controlled and progressive approach to training.

British Amateur Weight Lifters Association

All weight lifting in Great Britain is under control of the British Amateur Weight Lifters Association which is affiliated to the International Weight Lifting Federation and the British Olympic Association. The B.A.W.L.A. is responsible for coaching at all levels and maintains a National Coaching Scheme with a National Coach, assisted by staff coaches, senior coaches, coaches and instructors, and holders of the School Teachers Award. It is the responsibility of the Coaching Committee to ensure that the highest levels of training for lifters are achieved, through the qualification of coaches at the above levels. All lifters are most strongly advised to join an official B.A.W.L.A. club where they will receive first-class coaching by highly qualified coaches who have been trained on the basis of the information in this book. In this way their progress will be ensured, hopefully reaching the greatest heights of international competition. In addition, the B.A.W.L.A. is responsible for the training of a corps of referees of the highest standard and integrity and for the adjudication of all weight lifting at all levels.

Useful addresses

For further information on membership and all other activities of the B.A.W.L.A., lifters should contact the General Secretary:
W. Holland, O.B.E., F.A.D.O.
3 Iffley Turn
Oxford
or the National Coach, Director of Coaching and author of this book:
P. J. Lear, B.A., Dip. Phys. Ed.,
'The Willows',
4 Fords Heath,
Shrewsbury, Shropshire

Join the British Amateur Weight Lifters Association and participate fully in your chosen sport.

Conversion Table

1 kilogramme = 2.2046 pounds
For the purpose of recording weight lifting it is customary to convert to the nearest ¼ lb below.
e.g. 90 kg = 198.14 lb—198¼ lb

Range of poundage on the international bar bell:
1¼ kg = 2¾ lb;
2½ kg = 5½ lb;
   5 kg = 11 lb;
10 kg = 22 lb;
15 kg = 33 lb;
20 kg = 44 lb;
25 kg = 55 lb.

Bar bells with sleeves and collars 25 kg = 55 lb.

kilos	lb	kilos	lb	kilos	lb	kilos	lb
25	55	137½	303	250	551	362½	799
27½	61	140	308½	252½	556½	365	804½
30	66	142½	314	255	562	367½	810
32½	72	145	319½	257½	567½	370	815½
35	77	147½	325	260	573	372½	821
37½	83	150	330½	262½	578½	375	826½
40	88	152½	336	265	584	377½	832
42½	94	155	341½	267½	589½	380	837¾
45	99	157½	347	270	595	382½	843¼
47½	104½	160	352½	272½	600¾	385	848¾
50	110	162½	358	275	606¼	387½	854¼
52½	115½	165	363¾	277½	611¼	390	859¾
55	121¼	167½	369¼	280	617¼	392½	865¼
57½	126¾	171	374¾	282½	622¾	395	870¾
60	132¼	172½	380¼	285	628¼	397½	876¼
62½	137¾	175	385¾	287½	633¾	400	881¾
65	143¼	177½	391¼	290	639¼	402½	887¼
67½	148¾	180	396¾	292½	644¾	405	892¾
70	154¼	182½	402¼	295	650¼	407½	898¼
72½	159¾	185	407¾	297½	655¾	410	903¾
75	165¼	187½	413¼	300	661¼	412½	909¼
77½	170¾	190	418¾	302½	666¾	415	914¾
80	176¼	192½	424¼	305	672¼	417½	920¼
82½	181¾	195	429¾	307½	677¾	420	925¾
85	187¼	197½	435¼	310	683¼	422½	931¼
87½	192¾	200	440¾	312½	688¾	425	936¾
90	198¼	202½	446¼	315	694¼	427½	942¼
92½	203¾	205	451¾	317½	699¾	430	947¾
95	209¼	207½	457¼	320	705¼	432½	953¼
97½	214¾	210	462¾	322½	710¾	435	959
100	220¼	212½	468¼	325	716½	437½	964½
102½	225¾	215	473¾	327½	722	440	970
105	231¼	217½	479½	330	727½	442½	975½
107½	236¾	220	485	332½	733	445	981
110	241½	222½	490½	335	738½	447½	986½
112½	248	225	496	337½	744	450	992
115	253½	227½	501½	340	749½	452½	997½
117½	259	230	507	342½	755	455	1003
120	264½	232½	512½	345	760½	457½	1008½
122½	270	235	518	347½	766	460	1014
125	275½	237½	523½	350	771½	462½	1019½
127½	281	240	529	352½	777	465	1025
130	286½	242½	534½	355	782½	467½	1030½
132½	292	245	540	357½	788	470	1036
135	297½	247½	545½	360	793½		

Louis Martin MBE, Britain's greatest ever weight lifter: four times World Champion, four times Commonwealth Games Champion, World Record Holder, Bronze and Silver Olympic Medals.